SUICIDE TERRORISM—A SOLUTION

SUICIDE TERRORISM—A SOLUTION

ELDHO KOCHERY CHAKKAPPAN

PARTRIDGE

A Penguin Company

Partridge books may be ordered through booksellers or by contacting:

Partridge India
Penguin Books India Pvt.Ltd
11, Community Centre, Panchsheel Park, New Delhi 110017
India
www.partridgepublishing.com
Phone: 000.800.10062.62

CONTENTS

THIS BOOK IS DEDICATED TO MY FATHER,
THE LATE K.V. CHAKKAPPAN

AUTHOR'S NOTE

I T HAS BEEN more than a decade since the issue of suicide terrorism has been well and truly ingrained in my mind. As a practicing lawyer, I have seen many facets of the human mind with the twists and turns that take place when individuals go through trying situations and incidents in life. As a student of philosophy, the mindless violence of suicide terrorism and the apparent nonchalant attitude of the walk in suicide terrorists have baffled me.

In the many years that I have dwelled on the subject, the possibility of innocents being misled or misguided by indoctrination was considered by me as a hypothesis. It was with a view to put this concept to test that I decided to do a thesis with the Manchester University on this subject with dedicated research. I was extensively associated with the Manchester University from 2008 to 2009, before my thesis was accepted in November 2009.

Since then I have had many interactions with contemporary philosophers, modern liberals and my peer group on the thesis. While the content of the thesis was on sound footing, many did mention to me that the same was not easy reading for the general public.

The feedback from various quarters since the publishing of the thesis has been the driving force behind this book. In the first chapter I have tried to present the subject matter in a simplified manner for general reading. The approach of treating a suicide terrorist (or at least some of them) as an individual like you and me and looking at them with a humane approach may not be appealing to many of the readers. The content of truth in this book would be difficult to establish and some of you may even like to wish it away. The book is an effort to look at the problem of suicide terrorism in the eye. In the last chapter I have given a vision for philosophy in education curriculum. The book is an effort to provoke serious thinking on the culpability of suicide terrorists and to strengthen our education system to save many innocents, both for the suicide terrorists as well as the victims.

FOREWORD

By Justice V. Ramkumar

I FEEL PRIVILEGED IN being requested to write a foreword to this book titled "SUICIDE TERRORISM—A SOLUTION" brought out by Mr. Eldho, a resourceful lawyer who had captured my attention during the hearing of a church case. Chapters 2 to 8 of this book constitute the thesis which Mr. Eldho had presented before the University of Manchester. This thesis primarily focuses on the philosophy of 'culpability' and 'ignorance' of which the main exponents are Zimmerman, Gideon Rosen, Fitz Patric, Gurrero, Davidson, Strawson and Wallace. The topic has increasing relevance during these days of escalating terrorism. Mr. Eldho has a valid point in advocating the theory that Suicide Terrorism is not blameworthy in all cases. This commendable work raises the following issues and challenges:-

i) Whether an act of blameless moral ignorance can arise out of skewed religious brainwashing or misguided indoctrination?

ii) Is it permissible to equate blameless moral ignorance with the ignorance of an innocent child who is below the age of discretion so as to exempt the act from culpability?

iii) Whether conversion of otherwise useful citizens to suicide terrorists through indoctrination and constant brainwashing excuses the converter and the converted from the ordinary laws of the land which do not excuse the ignorant?

iv) Can suicide terrorism arising out of blameless ignorance can be compared to the act of a person non compos mentis who qualifies for the M'Naughten Rule?

v) Are well educated innocents craftily manipulated or habituated through institutionalized indoctrination to make them believe that they would gain glory in life after death and that their life has become meaningful through their death?

vi) Will glorification of martyrdom through skewed religious brainwashing attract volunteers to join terrorist organizations?

Mr. Eldho has stressed the need for re-structuring the curriculum in schools by including "philosophy" with a view to rekindling the thinking process in the children. Training persons in the entirety by educating the body, mind and imagination and thereby enabling them to have a holistic approach to logic is a reform recommended by the author for promoting creative thinking. A practitioner who is devoid of the ethics of his pursuits developing mercenary motives and eventually growing avaricious is a danger foreseen by the author if proper training and disciplining the body politic is not resorted to.

I am sure that this book will draw the attention of persons and personalities in all walks of life, young and old and has the potential of educating the readers. Let not the vulnerable minds of the gullible youth fall a prey to the sinister machinations of perverted and incorrigible souls among the terrorist organizations and imperil the moral, political, religious and communal fabric of democracies like India.

12.04.2011   **JUSTICE V. RAMKUMAR**

ACKNOWLEDGEMENT

FIRST AND FOREMOST, a big thanks to my wife Elizabeth. I wouldn't have even attempted writing this book or researching in Manchester if it was not for her wholehearted support. I know it was a mammoth sacrifice on her part to manage without having my presence for over two years.

To my children George and Sanjana. You have been the light of my life and will continue to be so.

To my Mother, Mariamma Chakkappan for being the most amazing lady I have ever known and for supporting me to study at this late stage.

To my brother Commander Kochery C. Shibu, the editor of this book. He very patiently listened to my suggestions and readily agreed to conduct innumerable brainstorming sessions with me on each and every topic. It was at his suggestion that we decided to keep the thesis as it is and include it verbatim in the book for the benefit of keen students of philosophy. The number of reviews on the first and last chapter, both in content and presentation, would not have been possible without his unrelenting support. I place on record my sincere thanks to David Liggins, Joel Smith and Peter Goldie of the University of Manchester, Department of Philosophy for all the inspiring discussions on the philosophical aspects of suicide terrorists which helped shape my thoughts in the approach to this book.

To my associate lawyers Jijo Thomas and Malleenathan, who effectively managed the office during my absence while I was away on my research work on the topic of this book and also to my associate Anesh Paul for his analytical skills in making this book more appealing.

To my brothers Dr Sabu, for his contributions on the research methodology and Ashok for his critical review of the book.

To Patridge, my publisher. I could not have asked for a better publishing team.

To Sreedevan Ramakrishnan, who took pains to read through each page of my work and for making suggestions on the same.

I place on record my sincere thanks to Shobha Menon, who supported me to write this book and to Ajith of Jitaads, for his immense help.

And last but definitely not the least to the Almighty. All this would not be possible without His guiding hand.

K.C. Eldho

CHAPTER 1

An Approach to Suicide Terrorism

I<small>T HAS ALWAYS</small> baffled me as to why well educated ordinary citizens become suicide terrorists. In the days that followed the infamous 9/11 attack of September 2001, there has been much outcry and heartburns. There were declarations of "global war on terrorism", with most of the world governments joining in. It is a matter of perception whether the elaborate efforts and money spent since then has made any dent in the number of innocents volunteering to be suicide bombers. One has to look beyond the standard prism to comprehend the phenomenon of suicide bomber. It is relatively easy to conclude that all the acts of suicide terrorism are blameworthy and one should condemn the same. The fact that the suicide bomber is the first casualty of his actions gives it a new dimension at the individual's level. Implicit is also that there is no material gain in the worldly life for the individual. Any conclusions pointing to the suicide bomber making a gain out of the act in the conventional sense also becomes irrelevant.

The legal system has an important part to play in the protection and maintenance of a just society while maintaining a holistic approach. The suicide terrorist by design gives up his life and by this very action, he is beyond the long arm of the law. It is not easy for an ordinary human being to kill himself and a number of innocent people along with him? How do they justify themselves? What emerges is the fierce strength of moral conviction and justification given to suicide terrorism, without which he cannot act as a suicide bomber. Convictions and beliefs form the backbone of the mental make up which is achieved through indoctrination and brainwashing. As it exists now the general approach of the media and the intelligentsia is to find every act of suicide terrorism blameworthy. This may not be true in all cases. It is well known that most societies treat misdeeds by children as not blameworthy, even though the deed itself may be blameworthy. This is also true in the case of misdeeds of a mentally ill person as he is not considered a rational human being. These may be clear cut cases in the theory on attributing blame. Can we extend the general theory on attributability of blame to include the suicide terrorists?

Holding someone culpable or not for an act, requires an in depth look with a historical review of the act. There after proceed to hold him culpable or otherwise. There is also the method of simulative analysis for clearer understanding before attributing blame. As a general principle, in all cases, we tend to attribute blame whenever there is a bad act that has taken place. Not much consideration is given to the possibility that a person could be blameless. Here comes the apparent paradox; can there be a bad act which is blameless?

The nuclear attacks and atomic bombings of Hiroshima and Nagasaki at the end of World War II were ordered by the US president Harry S. Truman against Imperial Japan in 1945. That the attacks with nuclear weapons in the war killed 140,000 in Hiroshima and 80,000 in Nagasaki by the end of 1945 is recorded history. There are thousands more who have died from radiation related diseases since then. It has been a matter of much debate whether the use of the nuclear bomb was necessary to achieve military victory against Japan, which seemed imminent even otherwise? Students of military history would know that the battle of Okinawa island of Japan was fierce with huge casualties on both sides in 1945. The invasion of Japan based on the experience would have been very costly in terms of human life on both sides. It is believed that Truman had given the decision after considering all the inputs that was available to him at that point in time. He believed that what he was doing was right, even though the act is considered to be a monumental wrong by many in the world.

The infamous second Gulf war is another example of such extreme situations. The invasion of Iraq by the multinational forces was led by troops from the United States under the administration of President George W. Bush and the United Kingdom under Prime Minister Tony Blair. The immediate cause for the attack was the belief of George W.

Bush that Iraq had weapons of mass destruction which was always a threat to the US and troops from other nations operating in the area.

After the attack, it emerged that Iraq had ended its nuclear, chemical and biological programs in 1991. There were no active programs at the time of the attack. The cost of the war to the Iraqis was huge. While the exact figures are not available, an estimate of 4.7 million refugees and 2.7 million internally displaced people has been reported in 2009. 35% of Iraqi children, or about five million children, became orphans. About 100,000 Iraqi civilians are believed to have died as a result of the war. The majority of deaths were due to violence, primarily as a result of U.S.-led military action (The Lancet 2004). The death due to suicide terrorist attacks all over the world would pale in front of this kind of apparent genocide.

The decision of George W. Bush to push for invasion on Iraq which has caused human suffering and death of such gigantic proportions was primarily based on his belief that Iraq was promoting weapons of mass destruction, especially chemical and biological ones. Can he be blamed for his act, even if we know today that it was indeed a bad act? If the answer is yes, the implication would be a war crime offence for crime against humanity. But then, the answer to date has been no. It is believed that he had acted based on inputs that were available to him at that point in time. Let us for a moment consider that he has been factually misled, or he was given partial truths by design or default; would he be culpable? The answer to all possibilities would still be no. The reason being that he is believed to have acted in good faith believing that he is right in his actions, based on inputs that were available to him, believing that he is doing the right thing.

Another extreme instance from history is the story of the Japanese civilians on Saipan Island during Second World War. (Historian Herbert Bix in "Hirohito and the Making of Modern Japan"). The allied forces invaded the island in 1944 and the military defeat of the Japanese troops defending the island was certain. The Emperor is believed to have issued an order to all Japanese civilians on Saipan to commit suicide. The order included the promise that, although the civilians were of low caste, their suicide would grant them a status in heaven equal to those honored soldiers who died in combat for their Emperor. In this lesser known event over 20,000 Japanese civilians jumped to their deaths from a cliff, many apparently in belief of the honour that would be bestowed upon them on dying.

There have been efforts to exonerate the Emperor from the responsibility of the orders since the Second World War. He has not been indicted in any of the war crimes. It is difficult for us to fathom the spirit of the Japanese civilians in the Saipan Island who decided to end their life to attain a greater status in the afterlife based on an apparent promise of the Emperor. The truth was supposedly furthering the fighting spirit and cause of the nation which has been achieved (to what ever little extent it did) by this promise to the civilians. Is the Emperor of the erstwhile Imperial Japan culpable for the deaths of these innocent civilians? The apparent answer has been 'no' till date. With the available information today, it is possible that the Emperor may have been blameworthy.

The philosophy on attributability of blame gives some interesting perspectives. The human tendency to blame anyone and everyone when things go wrong is well known. "We all love to blame," says Gideon Rosen. If we are not blaming each other, we are blaming the traffic or the weather. Praise and blame are glues that keep a society together. He also goes on to say that when you reflect on an act of yours which you think is wrong, you often come up with a story to assuage your feeling of guilt or remorse and tell yourself that you actually had no choice to act any other way. There are extraneous factors which often makes people feel that they cannot have moral responsibility. The concept of value system and moral responsibility is the privilege of the humans. There are situations when you are ignorant of the facts; and there may be decisions and actions which you have taken on facts that were available to you. In that case, though the outcome of your act is bad, you cannot be held to blame. Equally important is the concept of blameless moral ignorance. Here the focus is moral convictions and beliefs. If the individual is not culpable for ignorance on a certain issue, then he cannot be culpable for any actions arising out of the ignorance, provided his ignorance is not an upshot of negligence or recklessness. Then there is the all familiar self justification, wherein you know it is wrong and you go through all the arguments that tell you it is morally wrong but in self interest you think you should act otherwise.

Attributing of blame has also got social and legal perspectives. The legal system provides punishment for any act against law which makes the individual culpable. The framework of the legal system has been developed over the centuries and is meant to keep the society stable and a safe place. In its simplest form, it is a set of rules and a punishment system to deter offenders. The legal system across the nation states in the world is applicable to people when they are alive. There is no legal frame work existing to prosecute the dead. This assumes significance in the case of suicide terrorists who are not available for a trial under law. By the very same yard stick, the act of suicide terrorism itself becomes beyond the law and norms of society as we see it today. The punishment whether deterrent or reformative available in the legal system of each country is to curtail the misdeeds and to protect the life, property and liberty of the people of the state. All these measures are effective in so far as the living human beings are concerned. What about the suicide terrorist? Are we to break barriers and consider the philosophy of prosecuting the dead? As it stands now suicide terrorists are beyond law with death. It becomes all the more relevant to examine in depth the aspects of moral responsibility.

It is not always that the attribution of blame is clear cut black and white situation. In a similar vein, a bad act arising out of firm religious belief, will it be blameworthy? This assumes significance because of the very vast spectrum that it relates to. Misguided religious convictions can lead to bad acts where the individual may be acting out of moral ignorance. In such a case the individual is not blameworthy. There are also suicide terrorists who are acting out of blameless moral ignorance. These are mostly the so called "walk in suicide bombers" who have been manipulated by indoctrination by vested interests. Consequently it follows that they are not culpable for their act. The concept of blameless ignorance becomes hard to accept when we consider the gravity of the destruction and damage that may have been caused and the countless innocents who may also have lost their lives. There is a well established norm for attributing blame in all societies. There is near universal clarity in handling the instances of misdeeds by children where we conclude that the act of the child is not blameworthy as the child is acting out of blameless ignorance. The extension of the above principle to hold that a suicide terrorist is not culpable for the act if his act is one out of blameless ignorance becomes debatable. The question whether a suicide terrorist is acting out of blameless moral ignorance and hence not culpable requires special consideration. Can we extend the rationale of "justification based on beliefs and acting in good faith" as in the case of the invasion of Iraq to the suicide bomber. Their acts are also based on convictions and beliefs arising out of brainwashing or indoctrination. Can we therefore say that they are not culpable as the act is arising out of blameless moral ignorance?

In the cases of the nuclear attack of Hiroshima in 1945 and the invasion of Iraq in 2003, there has been huge loss of life to innocent civilians as also to property. Objective wrongness of these acts alone would bring in moral culpability to the agent. But as highlighted earlier, in both cases the action has been considered non culpable on grounds of blameless ignorance. Needless to say that tracing culpability of an act becomes very difficult as we are often kept in the dark regarding the precedents of the agent. Majority of the philosophers are of the view that establishing culpability of an act would depend on whether the individual was having knowledge as to whether the act was wrong or not. In instances where the individual had the knowledge of right and wrong as regards the act or options and still decided to go ahead with the wrong, then definitely he or she is culpable. In the case of the suicide terrorist, he believes what he is doing is right and is possibly the only right, and proceeds with that conviction. In such a case can we hold them culpable? Manipulative indoctrination is at the root of the misplaced conviction that is the driving force of many suicide terrorists.

Most of the walk-in suicide terrorists believe that what they are doing is righteous. Some of them even believe that they are destined to be suicide terrorists for a nobler cause. In such cases, the mental and moral disposition of the suicide bomber is to sacrifice his life in the act. How do they reach such extreme state of mental make up? This is achieved by institutionalized method of indoctrination, brainwash and skewed religious propaganda. Most of the suicide terrorists who give up their life with such commitment do so with firm conviction that they are righteous in their deed. At one end of the spectrum is the indoctrination that suicide bombers are subjected to which could be considered as brainwashing. Other end of the spectrum is manipulated indoctrination, that powerful tool which the perpetrators use to literally rewrite a persons beliefs and attitudes. The indoctrination of suicide bombers is that single tool which completely violates their value system, and gives a make over even to well educated people to become walk in suicide bombers.

There are many stereotyped perceptions doing the rounds on suicide bombers of which the most popular one is that they are crazy, insane, or irrational. Apparently their value system is different in many ways. But in most cases, they are not crazy from a standpoint of mental health. Another popular perception is that suicide bombers are driven by poverty and an 'unbearable present'. There may be some truth in this. This is so since many of their societies are quite poor. More often than not, suicide bombers themselves seem to be the better off ones even in their poor society.

The thesis which I did with the Manchester University is an effort to strike at the root of the malaise which has made many innocents into suicide terrorists. The vested interests in many parts of the world have institutionalized indoctrination as a sublime art. Even the apparently well educated innocents are also artfully manipulated and indoctrinated to believe that they would achieve glory in life after death and find meaning to their life by dying. These innocents are often not even aware of the ulterior motives and the political aim of the perpetrators.

The thesis primarily focuses on the philosophy of culpability and ignorance. The main exponents are Zimmerman, Gideon Rosen, Fitz Patric, Guerrero, Davidson, Strawson and Wallace. The thesis which I presented before the University of Manchester for my degree Master of Research is reproduced verbatim as chapter 2 to 8. Subsequent to the thesis I have considered various options to address the issue of suicide terrorism. I have given the way ahead in chapter 9 of this book. The suicide terrorist, by the very act of dying puts him beyond the reach of law as also the legal frame work in any modern nation state. Any deterrence that the policing and the legal system provide also turns out to be ineffective against the all powerful human mind. The root cause for suicide terrorism lies in the fierce manipulation of the human mind by indoctrination or false religious propaganda. The society needs to make some radical changes. The readers will find the way ahead in chapter 9 interesting.

CHAPTER 2

INTRODUCTION

Zacarias Moussaoui, an educated French Moroccan, lived close to Brixton Mosque, UK. He did Business Studies at the South Bank University where he kept company of young Muslims. Many of them narrated their personal accounts of the atrocities meted out to their family members in Bosnia and Chechnya. A religious Muslim, Zacarias Moussaoui used to visit Finsbury Park Mosque, North London. Here he attended sermons of Abu Hamsa by chance and was attracted to his powerful preaching. Abu Hamsa is a radical Muslim fundamentalist. He indoctrinates young innocent youth and brainwash them to become suicide terrorists on the religious belief of holy war or "Jihad". Assume that Zacarias Moussaoui too was brainwashed by Abu Hamsa. He became an ardent believer of the teachings on holy war or "Jihad" as interpreted and taught by Abu Hamsa. He believed these to be true religious belief. He believed in eternal life in the other world. He considered it righteous to act according to his beliefs. Zacarias Moussaoui volunteered to become a suicide terrorist in the name of holy war or "Jihad" as brainwashed by Abu Hamsa. Zacarias Moussaoui participated in the 9/11 terrorist attack on the United States. He was apprehended and was brought to trial. He was calm all through the trial. He expressed no feeling of guilt or remorse. He prayed "God curse America" and stated that he had acted on behalf of God.

We find Zacarias Moussaoui was acting under indoctrination or brainwash. Can we hold him culpable for the act? Is it not a case where he was acting out of moral ignorance which is blameless? Would it be fair on our part to blame one for an act out of blameless moral ignorance? Would this be true in the case of all suicide terrorists? Do they all act out of blameless moral ignorance? An agent acting out of ignorance whether factual or moral, he is culpable for the act only if he is culpable for the ignorance from which he acts (Rosen, 2003, p.64). Can this theory be extended to all cases and whether suicide terrorists also fall within the ambit of this theory? This is the essence of my thesis.

I proceed on the hypothesis that suicide terrorists are not culpable. In chapter three, I will discuss the views on culpability and ignorance. I will start with the well known view of Zimmerman. In cases where an agent acts out of ignorance, to hold the agent culpable for the act, it is necessary that the ignorance out of which he acts itself is culpable. According to Zimmerman, the conditions for culpable ignorance occur less frequently than is commonly supposed (Zimmerman, 1997, p.411). Zimmerman argues that in all cases culpability can be traced to the lack of ignorance i.e. an act which involves a belief on the part of the agent that he/she is doing something morally wrong. From Zimmerman, I will proceed to the views of Gideon Rosen. Rosen defends Zimmerman. Rosen argues that there are many instances when we act out of ignorance. In some cases we attribute blame and in some we do not. Take the case of a child stealing a candy bar from the shop. Though stealing is morally wrong we refrain from blaming a child. This we say is because the child is acting out of ignorance. Take another example where an agent is walking through the street with his nose in a book and collides with a pedestrian. Our immediate response is to say that he cannot be excused for his ignorance and his act is blameworthy. An act out of blameless ignorance cannot be culpable. Thus Rosen put forward his pairty thesis i.e. "whenever an agent acts from ignorance, whether factual or moral, he is culpable for the act only if he is culpable for the ignorance from which he acts" (Rosen, 2003, P.64). Rosen argues that if blameless ignorance on facts is plausibility as in the case of the child stealing a candy bar from the shop, blameless moral ignorance should also be plausibility. In support of his argument Rosen provides the example of the slave holder in ancient years, when it was considered an accepted norm to own slaves, which is something unimaginable today. In this chapter, I defend the views of Rosen and his theory of parity thesis. I will also elaborate my views in support of the theory of blameless ignorance given by Rosen. I have tried to widen the spectrum with more examples to defend Rosens's theory and to illuminate the same.

Chapter 4 deals with the objections to the views on culpability and ignorance. The major objections are raised by Fitzpatrick and Guerrero. Fitzpatrick has attacked the view of blameless ignorance as given by Rosen. To identify blameless ignorance and to hold one not culpable for the act, we have to find the causal history of the act. Establish that the ignorance is not one out of negligence and that it is not one against the agent's own better judgment. Acting against one's own better judgment is referred to as Akrasia. Acting against one's own considered judgment about what there is most reason for him to do is referred to as Clear-eyed Akrasia. According to Rosen's view, to hold one responsible for an act requires an episode of Clear-eyed Akrasia in the causal history of the act. Fitzpatrick has raised the main objection that it is difficult and may be not practical to trace the episode of Clear-eyed Akrasia in the causal history of the act. The answer to the objection of Fitzpatrick is given in this chapter. Apart from these there are two arguments in this chapter. The first one is that Fitzpatrick has not fully appreciated the conditions laid down by Rosen for blameless ignorance. The second one is that the view about 'epistemic obligations' to be performed by the agent as given by Rosen has not been seriously considered by Fitzpatrick. Epistemic obligations referred to by Rosen are the standing obligations to inform ourselves about matters relevant to the moral permissibility of our conduct: to look around, to reflect, and to seek advice and so on i.e. moral obligations governing the epistemic aspects of deliberation (Rosen, 2003, p.63).

Fitzpatrick admits that the experience of guilt or shame that we feel during an act is a good evidence of Akrasia. Thus I will argue that in effect Fitzpatrick is not attacking the theories of blameless (factual or moral) ignorance and the parity thesis as given by Rosen. I have elucidated my arguments with some interesting examples in this chapter. Guerrero proceeds on the basis that an agent is to be held culpable even if he is acting out of ignorance (Guerrero, 2007). I will give my views against the same in answer to the objections of Guerrero and in defense of Rosen. The example referred by Guerrero to attack the theories given by Rosen is weak and does not stand scrutiny.

In chapter 5, the possibility of blameless moral ignorance arising out of religious belief is elaborated. The example of Zacarias Moussaoui as explained in the opening paragraph of this introduction and similar such cases are discussed at length. The view that an act out of blameless moral ignorance can also arise out of religious belief and/or misguided indoctrination is the foundation of this book.

In chapter 6, possible reasons for blameless moral ignorance are analyzed. Fighting for the motherland against foreign invasion or occupation is possibly the single major cause. Events arising out of social and cultural restrictions and pressures form another major reason. Forceful inducement of drugs, mistaken verdict, social injustice etc. forms the third cause. Brainwash and indoctrination on religious belief, and blameless ignorance out of false belief form another major cause.

In chapter 7, suicide terrorism and blameless moral ignorance are discussed. The findings of Robert A. Pape in the book 'Dying to win' is referred to. He conducted factual research on 462 cases of suicide terrorists during the period 1980-2004. My argument that suicide terrorists are acting out of blameless (moral or factual) ignorance and hence are not culpable for the act is formulated in this chapter. This argument is based on the ground that suicide terrorists are either acting on religious indoctrination or on a patriotism-based act of dying for the country or a combination of both. In all these cases the suicide terrorist is acting out of blameless moral ignorance. It is unfair to blame them and I argue that they are not culpable for the act.

In chapter 8, I have given my conclusion that it is plausible that most of the suicide terrorists are acting out of blameless (moral or factual) ignorance, and therefore they are not culpable for their act and it is unfair to blame them.

CHAPTER 3

Culpability and Ignorance

In this chapter, I will discuss the views on culpability and ignorance. I will start with the well known view of Zimmerman. In cases where an agent acts out of ignorance, to hold the agent culpable for the act, it is necessary that the ignorance out of which he acts itself is culpable. According to Zimmerman, the conditions for culpable ignorance occur less frequently than is commonly supposed (Zimmerman, 1997, p.411). Zimmerman argues that in all cases culpability can be traced to the lack of ignorance i.e. an act which involves a belief on the part of the agent that he/she is doing something morally wrong. From Zimmerman I will proceed to the views of Gideon Rosen. Rosen defends Zimmerman. Rosen argues that there are many instances when we act out of ignorance. In some cases we attribute blame and in some we do not. Take the case of a child stealing a candy bar from the shop. Though stealing is morally wrong, we refrain from blaming a child. This we say is because the child is acting out of ignorance. Take another example where an agent is walking through the street with his nose in a book and collides with a pedestrian. Our immediate response is to say that he cannot be excused for his ignorance and his act is blameworthy. An act out of blameless ignorance cannot be culpable. Thus Rosen put forward his parity thesis i.e. whenever an agent acts from ignorance, whether factual or moral, he is culpable for the act only if he is culpable for the ignorance from which he acts (Rosen, 2003, P.64). Rosen argues that if blameless ignorance on facts is plausibility as in the case of the child stealing candy bar from the shop, blameless moral ignorance should also be plausibility. In support of his argument Rosen provides the example of the slave holder in ancient years, when it was considered an accepted norm to own slaves, which is something unimaginable today. In this chapter I defend the views of Rosen and his theory of parity thesis. I will elaborate my views in support of the theory of blameless ignorance given by Rosen. I have tried to widen the spectrum with more examples to defend Rosen's theory and to illuminate the same.

The etymological meaning of 'culpability' refers to blameworthiness, guilt, or wrongness of an act. The issue of culpability for acts arising out of ignorance goes well beyond the ordinary understanding of morality. In attributing moral responsibility it is only fair to consider whether the act is out of ignorance or not. Consider an act by an individual which is cruel or brutal from an objective point of view. Can we presume the individual is not culpable, if his act is out of ignorance? A typical example would be of a child taking candy bar from a shop. We hold that though stealing is wrong and blameworthy, it is to be excused when done by a child at the age of 5 or even less as he/ she is ignorant about it. The act is considered innocent.

According to Zimmerman, culpability requires a belief on the agent's part that he or she is doing something morally wrong. Thus for Zimmerman the conditions for culpable ignorance are pretty restrictive and that therefore culpable ignorance occurs less frequently, than is commonly supposed (Zimmerman, 1997, p.411). The ignorance that is directly relevant is the ignorance of the agent who is doing something morally wrong. Zimmerman explains his view through the example of Perry who rescues Dorris in a car accident. Perry finds the car driven by Dorris hits a tree and she is unconscious slumped over the steering wheel. Perry comes upon the scene. He looks around and finds no one in the area. Perry thinks of the car catching fire and feels that he should rescue her. Perry rushes and drags Dorris from the car. Perry ensures that they are far away from the car and he collapsed exhausted. The car did not explode as thought by Perry. Within a few minutes emergency vehicles come to the spot and paramedics jump out. Perry explains what happened. Paramedics take a look at Dorris and they arrive at a chilling conclusion: Perry has paralysed Dorris (Zimmerman, 1997, p.410). Is Perry culpable for paralyzing Dorris? Can Perry be blamed for being ignorant about the first aid to be given in case of a rescue operation? Is it wrong that Perry was ignorant about the fact that Dorris may go paralysed if she is dragged out from the car? As we see, there is no carelessness or inconsiderateness on the part of Perry in doing the act. Perry did not believe that he was being careless or inconsiderate. Assume that had he known better about first aid and the possibility of paralysis he would have acted better. But can we attribute the 'ought to have known better' in this case to hold Perry culpable? In this case the ignorance is present and Perry is acting out of ignorance and there is a consequential bad result where Dorris goes paralysed. According to Zimmerman, culpability for ignorant behaviour must involve a belief on the part of the agent that the agent is doing something morally wrong.

Zimmerman summarizes his view as follows:

> "If one is culpable for non ignorant behaviour, then of course one's culpability involves a lack of ignorance. If in contrast, one is culpable for ignorant behaviour, then one is culpable for the ignorance to which this behaviour may be traced. Hence one's culpability for one's ignorant behaviour, at least, is merely indirect. But one is never in direct control of whether one is ignorant. Hence one's culpability for one's ignorance is also merely indirect. Indirect culpability for something presupposes direct culpability for something else. Whatever this something else is, it cannot be ignorant behaviour because then the argument would apply all or again to this behaviour. Hence all culpability can be traced to the culpability that involves lack of ignorance, i.e. that involves a belief on the agent's part that he or she is doing something morally wrong" (Zimmerman,1997,p.418). Thus according to Zimmerman, lack of ignorance concerning wrong doing is a root requirement of responsibility. I will put it as follows i.e. to hold an agent responsible for wrong doing, the agent should have the knowledge that he or she is doing a wrong act. Gideon Rosen defends the arguments of Zimmerman.

According to Rosen, whenever an agent acts from ignorance whether factual or moral, he is culpable for the act only if he is culpable for the ignorance from which he acts (Rosen, 2003, p.64). Rosen explains his theory by giving examples including the one which I referred to in chapter one about the minor child taking a candy bar from the shop.

In the case of the minor child we absolve the responsibility of stealing a candy bar from the shop. This is since the child is not expected to know about morality of stealing a candy bar from the shop and is acting out of ignorance. We justify such ignorance and hold the child not culpable. The excuse goes to the innocence presumed with his or her infancy. The similar category of excuses is extensive in number. These include insanity, infancy, certain forms of coercion, necessity and so on. It is common knowledge that we do apply these excuses in some cases but not in all cases. In the case of the child we immediately excuse him/her for stealing, though stealing is considered wrong.

Let us analyze what happens in this process. We understand that the child is very young to know that it is stealing and therefore it is wrong. The child has to acquire knowledge about value systems and learn about right and wrong. This comes with age and the process of growing up of the child. The child has to grow up mentally and physically till he/she reaches the adult age. In the case of children almost all over the world this age is typically taken as 12 years, till that age we consider them innocent. What follows is that the infant or the child in this age, though doing a bad act, is actually acting out of ignorance and acting innocently.

According to Rosen, an act out of ignorance can be blameless in certain cases. He provides the example of trespassing. Consider a private property which is altogether unmarked adjacent to the public forest. An agent, who strays into the property in the course of his morning walk, is committing trespass. This is since the agent is using another's land without his permission. Trespassing is wrong, but in cases like this it will be wrong if the agent is blamed. The agent is ignorant about the fact that he is committing trespass. There is no evident boundary available to make the agent feel that he is trespassing into a private property. In the above case, had the agent known better he would have acted otherwise. The ignorance of the agent in not identifying the private property which is lying contiguous with the public forest cannot be construed as an upshot to recklessness, negligence or deliberate misconduct in the management of his opinion. Rosen further gives an example of an agent walking through a crowded street with his nose in a book and hit a pedestrian and say that he never knew that the pedestrian was there. We would immediately say "that is no excuse". The agent should have been careful and should have looked around and his ignorance is nothing but an upshot of recklessness or negligence. It thus becomes clear that there are instances where ignorances are blameless and some where they are blameworthy.

In trespassers example, the ignorance is not an outcome of carelessness, disregard or purposeful misconduct in the management of his opinion. In the second example where the agent is walking through the street with his nose in his book, the agent's carelessness is evident. The agent does have an obligation to look around and ensure that he is not causing injury to another on the street. If the agent shirks from that obligation and pleads ignorance, that ignorance by itself is not an excuse and is culpable.

To ensure the moral permissibility of our conduct we have to abide by obligations as well i.e. to look around, to reflect, and to seek advice and so on. Rosen calls this as 'epistemic obligations'. The phrase epistemic obligations, according to Rosen, are the moral obligations governing the epistemic aspects of deliberation (Rosen, 2003, p.63). Thus an act of an agent out of ignorance is considered blameless if he or she is neither negligent nor reckless in the management of his or her opinion. The act is blameless because the ignorance out of which the person acts is also blameless. On the other hand, if the agent is negligent or irresponsible in his epistemic conduct then he is culpable for the ignorance and the performance of the act out of such ignorance is equally culpable. Rosen derives the principle from the above as follows. 'An action done from non-culpable ignorance is itself non-culpable' (Rosen, 2003, p.64). The examples referred above are more concerned with ignorance of fact. Whether the above principle can be extended for generality needs further deliberation.

As in the case of ignorance of facts there can be cases of moral ignorance as well. There can be cases of individuals failing to know the general moral rule and individuals not knowing that certain acts are cruel and abusive. Not knowing about rights and duties of individuals. According to Rosen (2003, p.64),

"An action done from non-culpable ignorance is itself non-culpable holds in full generality".

This means that irrespective whether the ignorance is factual or moral, the agent is culpable for the act only if he is culpable for the ignorance from which he acts. Rosen calls this as parity thesis, i.e.

"Whenever an agent acts from ignorance whether factual or moral he is culpable for the act only if he is culpable for the ignorance from which he acts" (Rosen, 2003, p.64).

When the principle of parity thesis is extended to the area of moral ignorance, it is necessary that the possibility of blameless moral ignorance be proved. If the plausibility of blameless moral ignorance is not proved the theory of parity thesis is not on sound footing.

Rosen has come forward to argue that blameless moral ignorance is a possibility. He refers to an example of ancient slavery in support of his argument. That is to say blameless moral ignorance does exist. It is undisputed that human slavery is indeed very bad; equally so is the buying and selling of human beings. Can an ancient slave holder be blamed for not knowing that slavery is a bad act? In those days it was socially accepted. Now to find out whether this ignorance is blameless or not Rosen applies the principles, which are applied in the case of factual ignorance as referred to above. The slave holder is not acting against his own better judgment; he is also not acting against his considered judgment about what there is most reason for him to do. Acting against one's considered judgment about what there is most reason for him to do is referred to as Clear-eyed Akrasia. When the ignorance is not an outcome of epistemic irresponsibility, like carelessness or thoughtlessness in the management of one's opinion, the absence of Clear-eyed Akrasia, in the causal history of the act is evident. This would establish whether the act is one out of blameless moral ignorance or not. Experience of guilt or shame is a good evidence for Clear-eyed Akrasia. Acting against one's own better judgment is referred to as Akrasia. The word akrasia finds its origin from the Greek word 'kratos' and is usually meant for weakness of will. The literal English word for akrasia would be incontinence. Akrasia is usually referred to the condition in which, while knowing what would be the best thing to do one does something else. It is also a condition of weakness of will and a failure to act according to a sense of moral obligation. A case in point would be the quintessential smokers who know it is best for them to quit smoking but they do not. It is against their better judgement and a clear expression of weakness of will or Akrasia.

Davidson gives a classic definition of weakness of will or Akrasia. Consider the case of an agent doing an act b. The agent acts inconsistently or akratic if and only if:

a) The agent does b intentionally
b) The agent believes there is an alternative action open to him.
c) The agent judges that all things considered, it would be better to do a than to do b (Davidson, 1969, p.22).

Another example given by Rosen is the case of Smith (1952) who gave differential treatment to his daughters as against his sons. Smith doesn't know it is unfair and wrong. If he is asked about the same he would say without any guilt or shame "yes, because they are girls". Smith is not acting against his better judgment and his differential treatment is not malicious. Can Smith be blamed for his ignorance? The answer would be no. This is a case of acting out of moral ignorance. He was acting as per the social norms that prevailed in the society that he lived in, at that point in time, and it will be unfair to blame him.

Let us once again consider the case of the slave owner of the olden days. The slave holder is expected to meet the epistemic obligations. Did he act on what he has most reason to do? The social practices that prevailed and the intellectual and cultural resources available during the period were very different from those of today. Under the circumstances, the slave holder has not acted against his better judgment.

It is important to note that situations can also arise where an agent acts on a mistaken verdict but non akratic. One of the most controversial decisions of President Truman during World War II has been ordering nuclear bombing of Hiroshima and Nagasaki. Truman ought to have known about the possible consequences of nuclear bombing considering his moral view. Assume that Truman has considered all sides of the issue and after deliberating on the issue believed his act to be a right one. Truman acts in tune with his better judgment and order bombing in Hiroshima. Truman is not strictly culpable for his act though the act was monumentally wrong (Rosen, 2003, p.69).

Rosen thus takes us a step further to show that the gravity of the bad act has got nothing to do with the theory he puts forward to hold one culpable or not culpable. Parity thesis can be made equally applicable in most cases and move towards generality. Culpability requires an episode of Clear-eyed Akrasia in the absence of which it is hard to hold an agent culpable. There are many instances where people act out of moral ignorance. The examples I have referred above show the possibility of the existence of blameless moral ignorance. If blameless moral ignorance is a possibility, then parity thesis is to be true. I will defend the argument that blameless moral ignorance is a possibility and parity thesis is true and I will defend the theory of Rosen as against the objections raised against his theory. In all the cases referred, the agent is blamelessly ignorant of a moral truth because the route to that truth is difficult for him to reach. This has given his starting point irrespective of the fact that he does everything typically required of him. Take the case of the slave holder; even if he put in all his efforts, it is impossible for him to find the moral truth of holding slaves as wrong (as we see today) because of cultural and social factors that existed in those times. Moral blame is more like a psychic punishment or a form of adverse treatment. In certain cases we find blame is appropriate and in certain cases it would be a mistake. Moral norms are generally used as the gauging factor for blame. We usually attribute blame using the norms of fairness. According to Jay Wallace, two important norms of fairness governing blame are:

> It is unfair to blame someone for doing something if he was morally entitled to do it. It is unfair to blame someone for doing something if at the time he (blamelessly) lacked the general capacity to appreciate and to act on the moral reasons for doing otherwise (Wallace, 1994).

According to Rosen, the principles do not explain the standard justifications and excuses. It does not cover the cases like the slave holder, Smith and Truman. I will argue that Rosen is right in not accepting the principles of Jay Wallace.

There would be no example more apt than the Spanish Inquisition which lasted for nearly 350 years. The Spanish Inquisition officially started in the mid-to late-fourteen hundreds. The Spanish Inquisition was a country-wide persecution of Jews for which there are several different reasons as to why it began. The actual reason, or reasons, that motivated the King and the Queen are still not known. Those who did the persecuting and the killing of the Jews were called Inquisitors. These people did not mind doing the killing or torturing. Some thought that the Jews were causing sicknesses and the Black Plague. Others thought that what they were doing was God's work: It has been said that the zealots of the Inquisition, even in their greatest cruelty, believed themselves to be justified in what they did. We are asked to accept as a fact that they were deeply religious men who honestly and sincerely believed that they were serving God in what they did. We are told that they believed Jews were destined for damnation, and that it was their duty to save them from that no matter what pain they inflicted on the bodies of the Jews here on Earth (Peters, E., 1989)

The Inquisitors believed that they were saving the Jews for a hideous fate in the Underworld. They believed that since the Jews were dying at the hands of one of God's children who were a follower of God, they would get the wisdom and knowledge of this person, and therefore go to heaven. Although now, this may be incomprehensible, at the time of the Inquisition, the Inquisitors were not educated in any manner other than a religious one, and had become highly religious individuals. This added up to what we would now call blind faith. This means believing in something for no reason other than religious custom or tradition.

Take the example of performing 'Sati'. It was the Hindu religious belief that the widow is best off by burning herself to death in the funeral pyre of her husband. Performing Sati or supporting the performance of Sati cannot come under the area where they are morally entitled to do it. It can also be not true to say that they blamelessly lacked the general capacity to appreciate and to act on the moral reasons for doing otherwise because a woman is burned alive and is supported and promoted on the ground of a religious belief.

Rosen provides a better principle on fairness as follows:

> "It is unfair to blame someone for doing something if he blamelessly believes that there is no compelling moral reason not to do it" (Rosen, 2003, p.74).

Rosen explains the above principle as supported by two more basic principles. It is unreasonable to expect people not to do what they blamelessly believe they are entitled to do. It is also unreasonable to subject people to sanction when it would be unreasonable to expect them to have acted differently. The principle of fairness advanced by Rosen appears to be more appealing as it covers a wider spectrum of cases falling under blameless moral ignorance.

Typically any agent who does a bad act will also have an excuse or justification for doing the same. If the agent is exonerated from attribution of moral responsibility on the basis of his justification, pleading ignorance and excuses, then no one will be culpable for their bad acts. It is here that the principles given by Rosen gains importance. Rosen provides a condition in cases where the agent acts from blameless moral ignorance that the ignorance itself is to be non culpable. It is further laid down that the ignorance should not be an upshot of recklessness or negligence or deliberate misconduct in the management of one's opinion. Thus applying the parity thesis of Rosen it arises that blameless moral ignorance is a possibility. It will be unfair to blame an agent for a bad act if it is an action out of blameless moral ignorance. We have to hold the slave owner of yester years as not culpable since his act is one out of blameless moral ignorance. The Spanish inquisitors who have done barbaric acts out of moral ignorance are also to be held non culpable. This is so in the case of Smith who differentiates the female children against the male ones. To emphasize the possibility of blameless moral ignorance I have already cited the example of 'Sati' as it existed in ancient India. Performing 'Sati' was considered as a pious ritual among Hindus in ancient India. The act is performed in the presence of all the relatives who support the performance of Sati as a ritual. The non performance of 'Sati' was considered to be an act against religious faith. Can the agent be blamed for performing 'Sati'? Can the relatives who support and encourage the performance of 'Sati' be blamed? Can moral responsibility be attributed to them? I would say no! The act is out of ignorance and that ignorance is not an upshot of recklessness or negligence or deliberate misconduct and hence is a case of blameless moral ignorance and the agent is not culpable for the act.

Another example is the practice of untouchability that existed in ancient India as a part of Hindu religious beliefs. Varnashram Dharma provided the social foundation of Hinduism. Four fold division of society according to social roles and status by the Hindus is known as the Varna system. The four Varnas are Brahmin, Kshatriya, Vaishya and Sudra. Among the four, Brahmin is considered as supreme and they are priests. It was the Brahmins who prescribed the duties of Hindus according to their Varnas. The Kshatriya had to provide state support to the Brahmins for the maintenance of the Hindu religion. The Vaishyas were to supply money and material goods according to the prescriptions of the Brahmins. Sudras were not given any religious prescription and they were treated as untouchables by the Brahmins. In ancient India, while a Brahmin was walking on the road all the Sudras were to move out of sight. This too was taken for granted as it is a religious belief. The discriminatory act of untouchability practiced in those days was socially accepted as a part of religious belief. The higher caste member treating the lower caste as untouchable was accepted by the society (Sharma, R, 1982, p.192). The act of the higher caste member in treating the lower caste member as untouchable is not an outcome of irresponsibility or carelessness or deliberate misconduct in the management of his opinion. Even if someone were to be asked in those days, the Brahmin would definitely say 'yes' it is only because they are Sudras and are to be treated as untouchables. There is no Clear-eyed Akrasia in the causal precedent of the act and the act is a non akratic one. It is one out of blameless moral ignorance and hence not culpable.

Brainwash and indoctrination is another area where blameless ignorance becomes a possibility. It is plausible that an agent X is brainwashed by Y and the indoctrination is such that the agent believes in the teachings of Y as truth and act out of the same. The agent never feels guilt nor is he shameful of his act. There is no clear-eyed Akrasia. The agent is not acting against his better judgment. The act comes within the arena of blameless moral ignorance and hence not culpable. The existence of blameless moral ignorance exonerates the agent from moral responsibility. Rosen relies on the existence of Akrasia in the causal history of an act to hold the agent responsible or culpable for the act. According to Rosen, an akratic agent is not acting out of ignorance. He knows that morally righteous would be to do 'A'. His moral reasons are compelling, and all things considered A is the right thing to do. He still can't bring himself to do A and does something else. In this case the act is not from ignorance and is not to be excused (Rosen, 2003, p.83). Here Rosen refers to a considered judgment, which is Clear-eyed Akrasia i.e. acting against one's considered judgment about what there is most reason for him to do. In the case of the ancient slave holder, if we are to ask him, he will definitely say that he does not feel guilty or shame in holding slaves. In those days it was a part of the value system, and the landed gentry used to pride on the number of slaves they owned. Applying the principles laid down by Rosen for blameless factual ignorance, the act of the slave holder is nothing but blameless moral ignorance and he is not culpable for the act.

Essence of Rosen's view can be taken as two fold. Firstly, to hold an agent culpable of an action, an instance of genuine Akrasia must be present in the causal history of that action. Secondly, we do not have enough grounds to judge an action as akratic or not. It would be apt to say that in Rosen's view culpability requires presence of Akrasia in the causal history of an act. An agent is culpable for performing the wrong action A only if he consciously judges that A is wrong when he elects to perform A.

CHAPTER 4

OBJECTIONS TO ROSEN'S VIEW ON CULPABILITY
AND IGNORANCE—AN ANALYSIS

IN THIS CHAPTER, I will consider the objections to the views on Culpability and Ignorance. The major objections are raised by Fitzpatrick and Guerrero. Fitzpatrick has attacked the view of blameless ignorance as given by Rosen. To identify blameless ignorance and to hold one not culpable for an act, we have to find the causal history of the act. Establish that the ignorance is not one out of negligence and that it is not one against the agent's own better judgment. Acting against one's own better judgment is referred to as Akrasia. Acting against one's own considered judgment about what there is most reason for him to do is referred to as Clear-eyed Akrasia. According to Rosen's view, to hold one responsible for an act requires an episode of Clear-eyed Akrasia in the causal history of the act (Rosen, 2004). Fitzpatrick has raised the main objection that it is difficult and may not be practical to trace the episode of Clear-eyed Akrasia in the causal history of the act. I will be giving my explanation in answer to the objection of Fitzpatrick in this chapter. I will argue that Fitzpatrick has not fully appreciated the conditions laid down by Rosen for blameless ignorance. The view about epistemic obligations to be performed by the agent as given by Rosen has not been seriously considered by Fitzpatrick. Epistemic obligations referred to by Rosen are the moral responsibility of our conduct. This means to look around, to reflect, and to seek advice and so on. Fitzpatrick admits that the experience of guilt or shame that we feel during an act is a good evidence of Akrasia. Thus I argue that in effect Fitzpatrick is not attacking the theories of blameless (factual or moral) ignorance and the parity thesis as given by Rosen. I am elucidating my case with some interesting examples in this chapter. Guerrero proceeds on the basis that an agent is to be held culpable even if he is acting out of ignorance. I will give my explanation against the same in answer to the objections of Guerrero and in defense of Rosen. The example referred by Guerrero to attack the theories given by Rosen is weak and does not stand scrutiny.

The major objections against blameless moral ignorance are raised by Fitzpatrick. According to Fitzpatrick, if the agent X is to be held responsible for an act A, then either act A itself is to be a Clear-eyed Akrasia or it results from such Akrasia associated with A's causal history. But it is not possible for us to know in any particular case whether such Clear-eyed Akrasia is really involved in the etiology of the action. Therefore it is not possible to know in any particular case whether X is truly responsible for A and we should suspend our judgment about it. Fitzpatrick provides the following argument to show that it is not possible to know in any particular case whether the agent is truly responsible for the act. i) If an agent X is responsible for a wrong act A, either a) X is "originally responsible" for A, or b) X is "derivatively responsible" for A by virtue of being originally responsible for something else that lead to A. ii) Thus, "if X is responsible for A then either a) A itself is a locus of original responsibility or b) There exists such a locus of original responsibility somewhere in A's causal history". iii) 'A' can be a locus of original responsibility (case ii.a above) only if X knows the balance of reasons against doing A; ignorance of this—whether due to circumstantial ignorance or due to normative ignorance—removes original responsibility for A. iv) Thus, X will be originally responsible for A only if his action is a case of Clear-eyed Akrasia (i.e. acting against his considered judgment about what there is most reason for him to do). v) If instead X is ignorant of the balance of reasons against doing A, and hence is not originally responsible for A, then X may still be derivatively responsible for A (case i.b above) but only if X is culpable for the relevant circumstantial or normative ignorance by being originally responsible for whatever led to that state of ignorance. vi)But (as in iii) X will be originally responsible for what led to his ignorance only if this amounted to a knowing failure to fulfill certain procedural epistemic duties—i.e., knowing "negligence or recklessness in the management of his opinion", in this case related to securing knowledge of the balance of reasons against doing A. (Otherwise, if X has been duly thoughtful and reflective all along, and his ignorance is merely a result of poor available information, bad upbringing, or being in the grip of a false normative view despite his best effort, then the ignorance leading to X to do A is not his fault: he blamelessly believes what he believes). vii) So the only way for X to be responsible for what lead to the ignorance that resulted in A would again be for X to have been involved in a form of Clear-eyed Akrasia in connection with the relevant epistemic ally debilitating behaviour—i.e., knowing that he had most reason to fulfill certain epistemic duties and yet failing to do so, knowingly being negligent in the management of his opinion. viii) Thus, if X is responsible for A, then either A is itself a case of Clear-eyed Akrasia or it results from such Akrasia associated with A's causal antecedents. ix) But it is not possible for us to know in any particular case whether such Clear-eyed Akrasia is really involved in the etiology of the action. x) Therefore it is not possible to know in any particular case whether X is truly responsible for A, we should thus suspend judgment about it.

(Fitzpatrick, 2008, p.591-592).

The above argument of Fitzpatrick appears to be an attempt to show that it is impossible to identify Clear-eyed Akrasia. Upto step viii, the argument stands more appealing. But when it comes to step ix, it seems to be a direct jump to the conclusion that it is not possible for us to know in any particular case whether there is Clear-eyed Akrasia or it results from such Akrasia associated with A's causal history. Similarly, in step x which is relying on step ix, Fitzpatrick concludes that it is not possible to know in any particular case whether X is truly responsible for A and that we should suspend our judgment about it. I would argue that step ix and step x of the argument is not supported by cogent reasons and hence the conclusion in step x is wrong. It is interesting to note that Fitzpatrick is not attacking the theories of blameless moral ignorance and parity thesis of Rosen. Fitzpatrick is more on the apprehension that how we identify the relevant episode of Clear-eyed Akrasia. Fitzpatrick admits that in cases where agents are akratic they are responsible for the act. According to him, one form of evidence for Akrasia is the experience of guilt or shame that we feel even while acting. The presence of guilt or shame at the time of acting is therefore often good evidence of Akrasia which diminishes the plausibility of general skepticism about attributions of Akrasia (Fitzpatrick, 2008, p.595).

Fitzpatrick objects the theory of Rosen on blameless moral ignorance on the ground that it is difficult or near impossible to trace the causal history of the agent to understand whether the ignorance out of which the agent is acting is blameless or not. Rosen's view is that the agent is culpable for the act only if the agent is not acting out of blameless moral ignorance. I would argue that Fitzpatrick has not effectively considered or analyzed the scope of epistemic obligations as given by Rosen. An agent who pleads for the ignorance of the act without discharging his epistemic obligations is culpable for the act as the ignorance itself is culpable.

Distinguishing Clear-eyed Akrasia from 'imposters' is another area of objection of Fitzpatrick. According to Fitzpatrick, Rosen refers this as an ordinary weakness of will. When an agent loses confidence in the correctness of his prior normative knowledge, he changes his normative averment such that he favours a bad action. Fitzpatrick cites the example of Eric Poechlman who committed scientific fraud at the University of Vermont; by altering data, he claimed in the court that he is doing the right thing given all the people in his lab depending on him for salaries and the need to secure grants to pay those salaries. According to Fitzpatrick, this is not an example of weakness of will as used by Rosen but it is a weakness of conviction. Another potential imposter, according to Fitzpatrick, is a failure to access one's relevant normative knowledge at the time of acting. This is so since the agent acts in ignorance even though the balance of reasons is against the action. Fitzpatrick emphasize the objection against identifying an episode against Clear-eyed Akrasia by quoting the following observations of Rosen (2004, p.309):

'The real limitation on our access to underlying histories of human actions and to the states of knowledge and opinion that underlie them'

'God or a super psychologist might confidently identify an episode of genuine akrasia'

In other words, it is the skeptical worries on moral responsibility which is being attacked than the theory put forward by Rosen. I will defend Rosen on his theory of attributing culpability only in an akratic act. The main objection of Fitzpatrick against Rosen is that it is plausible to have moral responsibility even in the absence of Akrasia. For example, culpable non akratic exercise of vices such as over confidence, arrogance, dismissiveness, laziness, dogmatism, incuriosity, self indulgence, contempt and so on (Fitzpatrick,2008,p.609). As against this I will argue that these are again areas which fall under the category of not discharging the epistemic obligations as provided by Rosen and are culpable ignorance by itself and cannot be excused from the responsibility. When the ignorance itself is culpable, as it is one out of the failure to discharge the epistemic obligations, the episode of Clear-eyed Akrasia need not be further located to hold the agent culpable for the act. Thus the argument of Fitzpatrick that the tight linking of moral responsibility to Akrasia should be resisted does not merit consideration. It may be true that there are difficult cases where confusion could arise with regard to culpability by applying the theory of Rosen. But I will argue that the theory of Rosen on blameless moral ignorance and parity thesis will apply in the same way to all cases irrespective of the gravity of the act and appeals for generality.

Fitzpatrick admits that if an agent honestly discloses the episode of Clear-eyed Akrasia in an act, it is easy for holding the agent responsible for the act. The worry of Fitzpatrick appears to be that we are unable to locate the akratic episode in the causal history of the act of the agent to hold him culpable. I would meet this by a counter argument i.e. there may be a number of cases where the agent does a bad act but the same will never be known or reveal people and those agents are never blamed. For example:

> A is the wife of a wealthy man B. Assume A is more interested in the wealth of B than him as a husband. With the intention of acquiring B's wealth, A gives low dosage of poison to B and over a period of say two years, B dies and the death appears to be normal among public. A has consequently inherited the wealth of B.
>
> In this kind of a case, we cannot attribute culpability to A unless she reveals her bad act which is akratic. So I would argue that the difficulty in locating the episode of Clear-eyed Akrasia or our limitations to locate the same do not defeat the theory put forward by Rosen. The possibility of bad acts as referred above can be a reason for Rosen to observe that God or a super psychologist might confidently identify an episode of genuine Akrasia (Rosen, 2004, p.309).

Now take the example of the child taking candy bar from the shop. Suppose I give the name of the child as Mary. Now suppose we hear that a certain Mary has taken a candy bar from the shop without the knowledge of the shop keeper, we immediately tend to blame her and attribute culpability for the act. Later we are informed that she is a small child, and then the culpability issue immediately dissipates. Thus irrespective of our knowledge the act remains the same. Therefore a culpable act will remain culpable and equally so a non culpable act, irrespective of our attribution. To hold someone culpable for an act is as good as giving a psychic punishment or a form of adverse treatment. So is it fair to blame someone without making sure that you are not punishing an innocent? I would argue that it is here that the theory of Rosen gains relevance as he provides a tight linking of moral responsibility to Akrasia.

Fitzpatrick argues for an alternative view that appeals to facts about personal capabilities, social opportunities for acquiring normative knowledge and the role of voluntary exercise of vices in certain failures to fulfill epistemic obligations. According to him an agent is culpable for an act if:

> There were no limitations in his social contacts or in his capabilities that should have made the necessary broader reflection and information gathering impossible or unreasonably difficult for him'.
>
> 'The failure of adequate reflection and information gathering was instead the result of voluntary exercise of vices such as over confidence, arrogance, dismissiveness, laziness, dogmatism, incuriosity, self indulgence, contempt and so on'.
>
> 'He could have reasonably been expected to take steps that would have eliminated that ignorance, by refraining from exercising those vices and instead of taking advantage of the epistemically relevant opportunities available to him' (Fitzpatrick, 2008, p.605).

Though Fitzpatrick provides the above factors for confidently attributing responsibility even in the absence of Akrasia he himself concede that it is not sufficient to meet Rosen's theory. He apprehends that the appeal to the vices referred to him above will not give any result unless the exercise of these vices itself is culpable or not. This again takes us back to the worries about ignorance.

Fitzpatrick concede that cases of brainwashing and indoctrination is so extreme that a person could not reasonably have been expected to gain relevant normative knowledge and exhibited no culpable vice at any stage in failing to take steps to get it and hence cannot be held responsible. Similarly, to blame certain people for practices even though non-relativistically wrong as it seems plausible that there are cultural and historical context where the relevant knowledge is not reasonably available

(Fitzpatrick, 2008, p.612). According to me, though Fitzpatrick has made an attempt to attack the theory of Rosen, I have given sufficient explanation and argument to show that the objection of Fitzpatrick is not justified. I would add that the admission made by Fitzpatrick is also to be read as part of my argument against the objection of Fitzpatrick. To illuminate that Rosen's theory holds good, I quote the following observation of Fitzpatrick. The basic capabilities of an agent in his given social circumstances will have its own limitation for that agent to acquire relevant knowledge. We can only expect that limited knowledge. It is interesting to note that Fitzpatrick admits this position and he admires Rosen as follows.

"A virtue of Rosen's argument is that it alerts us to all of this, as well as to the plausible implication that, in such cases, it will not be one's fault if one comes to an incorrect, factual and/ or moral understanding may just never come to seem to one and so one cannot reasonably blame for it" (Fitzpatrick, P. 612).

I think that I have defended the theory of Rosen as against the objection of Fitzpatrick by giving reasonable explanation and arguments. I would hold that the objection of Fitzpatrick has not shaken the foundation of Rosen's theory.

Guerrero raised the following objections against the theory of Rosen. Guerrero proceeds on the basis that an agent is to be held culpable even if he is acting out of ignorance. Thus the attack of Guerrero is against the theory of blameless moral ignorance given by Rosen. Guerrero argues against the ignorant thesis which he calls IT, which refers to the theory of Rosen, i.e. whenever an agent acts from ignorance whether factual or moral he is culpable for the act only if he is culpable for the ignorance from which he acts. Guerrero proceeds on the premise that an agent may do a bad act from ignorance. She may not be culpable from the ignorance from which she acts, but she is culpable for the act.

In support of the above proposition Guerrero provides the example of the President who signs or vetoes a particular piece of legislation after obtaining necessary inputs from all the experts in the field. The President takes a decision and the consequential effect was adverse. In the case of the President, she knows that in deciding whether to sign or veto the piece of legislation she is motivated only by a desire to do what is right. She collects opinion from experts in all fields, deliberates and decides to sign the legislation. She decides so believing that she is morally right in doing so. Suppose it turns out that she is wrong. Assume the reasons were complicated and beyond the anticipation of the experts. Guerrero considers this as a case of an act from moral ignorance and it is blameless. Guerrero proceeds to compare the above case with that of the slave holder who owns a slave in ancient days as given by Rosen in support of his argument for blameless moral ignorance. Guerrero proposes three situations for an act out of ignorance or someone could be ignorant of some fact F as follows:

> "(11) Cases in which a person is ignorant because she has never thought about the issue (and so has no beliefs about F or only has unexamined 'implicit' beliefs about F).
>
> (12) Cases in which a person is ignorant because, though she has thought about the issue she has come to have false beliefs about F (she believes that not-F when in fact F).
>
> (13) Cases in which a person is ignorant, though she has thought about the issue, she doesn't know what to believe (she doesn't believe that F or that not-F)".

Guerrero argues that Rosen is relying on the first proposition above where the agent has never thought of the issue. He proceeds to say that the case of the slave holder as given by Rosen may fit into the second proposition 12. Guerrero finds that in the first two premises the agent doesn't know F and also doesn't know that one doesn't know.

I will argue that Guerrero is not correct in identifying the case of the slave holder given by Rosen as fitting into the second premise given by him on the following reasons.

The slave holder's case is not a case which comes under false belief. It is more a reflection of the social and cultural environment that existed in those days. This limited the agent acquiring the knowledge of the wrongness of the act even if he so wished to. In ancient days owning slaves was an accepted norm and with no wrong in it. Given the social and cultural practices of ancient days, to find holding slaves as wrong and blameworthy, the agent has to be a moral genius. The crucial question could be whether the act of holding slaves is an akratic one or not. As there is no evidence for Clear-eyed Akrasia, the act is nothing but a non akratic one and hence not culpable. Hence the proposition given by Guerrero as against the slave holder does not seem to be correct. The second premise i.e. 12 given by Guerrero that the agent not only does not know F but also doesn't know that she doesn't know is abstract and vague. Is it plausible for us to have knowledge about our ignorance which we do not know? The third premise 13 though appealing I will resist the same to consider it for culpability factor as given by Rosen. Guerrero, by applying the premise 12, has argued that the case of the President signing or vetoing the legislation falls within the ambit of that premise. I have already explained in chapter 2 with regard to the factual possibility of holding slaves as an act out of blameless moral ignorance. During the biblical period and ancient years slavery has been in existence. It was never considered as morally wrong to hold slaves. The argument against slavery and slave holding as given by Guerrero stands outside the ambit of philosophical debate. The argument of Guerrero that the slave holder is not acting from ignorance but he is acting in ignorance appears to be on the ground that the slave holder does not possess the true belief that slavery is wrong. I will resist this argument on the following reasons. When we say acting in ignorance, it implies the knowledge of our ignorance. If that is so, presence of Clear-eyed Akrasia is evident i.e. we know that we are ignorant about a certain belief or truth. Still we act, in such an event we are culpable for the act. Another important aspect is that is it ever possible for an agent to act in ignorance. Is it not a logical fallacy? Suppose the slave holder says that he is ignorant whether holding slaves is wrong or not. But he still holds slaves for his convenience, benefit or enjoyment. In such a case of course what Guerrero argues may be true. But the case of the slave holder and the case of Smith, the American sexist as given by Rosen, is totally on a different footing. The slave holder of Rosen is one who holds the slaves believing that he is right to hold slaves. So is the case of Smith. He finds nothing wrong in differentiating the female children as against the male. Rosen refers to the social and cultural factors that existed in those days. This forms the reason for arguing that their act is out of blameless moral ignorance. I will argue that the aforesaid argument against Rosen is not only weak but also incorrect. The case of the President cannot be compared with the case of the slave holder. The case of the President as explained by Guerrero is a case of mistaken verdict as rightly referred to by Rosen in the case of Truman issuing order to bomb Hiroshima. It is a case of taking a decision after considering all inputs. As the example of the President as given by Guerrero is not comparable as such, the argument based on the same cannot be accepted. It further appears that Guerrero is exploring on the factual possibility and cultural datas of ancient slave holders to meet the philosophical argument of Rosen on culpability and ignorance.

Guerrero argues that there are cases in which an agent acting from ignorance seems culpable. He provides the example of a dog sitter in support of his argument. The dog sitter falsely believes that dogs cannot feel pain because he has read Descartes and believes that non human animals are no more than automata, intricate machines, and that machines cannot feel pain. The dog sitter is rolling a heavy wheel barrow through the garage into the yard. He finds that the wheel barrow may roll over the tail of the dog. He falsely believes that dogs do not feel pain. He continues to roll the wheel barrow and the dog appears in great pain. On the basis of the above example Guerrero argues that an agent acting out of ignorance can be culpable for the act. He further moves to argue for including the case of the slave holder as a case wherein the slave holder is culpable though he is acting out of ignorance.

I oppose this view on the following reasons. Rosen does not argue that all acts out of ignorance are not culpable. Only those acts which are non-akratic alone come within the purview of non-culpable acts. In the case of the slave holder, Rosen refers to the social and cultural environment as then existed which caused limitations to the slave holder to attain the relevant knowledge. Rosen provides an example of an agent who is walking through the street with his nose in his book and hits a pedestrian. In this example of the street walker, Rosen explains the culpability of the act though acting in ignorance. The ignorance of the street walker by itself is culpable and hence the consequential act is equally culpable. In the dog sitter's case, the ignorance by itself is culpable as he failed to perform the epistemic obligations as provided by Rosen and hence the consequential act is also equally culpable. I will argue that the dog sitter's case of Guerrero is not a case comparable with that of the slave holder. Guerrero also challenges the scope of epistemic obligations as provided by Rosen. Guerrero further argues that there can be variations in the depth of epistemic obligations. According to him, the slave holder ought to have thought about the wrongness of holding slaves. The performance of epistemic obligation should have given the hindsight to the slave holder to know that the act of holding slaves is wrong. If this argument of Guerrero is accepted then we will have to hold that the slave holder ought to have been a moral genius. It is less clear as to why Guerrero has argued to such an extent. He has tried to re-visit the cultural and social limitations that existed during the period of ancient slavery for acquiring relevant knowledge. Guerrero finally sums up to hold that the slave holder is culpable for the act. I hardly find any material or cogent reason in support of his contention as explained.

Guerrero provides a counter example to the moral ignorance thesis. It is the case of Douglas who is contemplating to kill a pig for dinner. Douglas is thinking whether the pig has a moral status or not. If he knew that the pig did have a significant moral status he would not kill it. Douglas is uncertain whether the pig has a moral status or not. Douglas does have reasons for wanting to kill and eat the pig as he liked the taste. Though he is unable to decide the moral status of the pig, he goes ahead to kill and eat it. In this case, is Douglas acting from ignorance? If so, is he culpable for his ignorance and culpable for the consequential act of killing the pig? Guerrero raises the above example in support of his argument.

If it is indeed true that pigs have a significant moral status, then Douglas is acting from ignorance. If it is false, still Douglas is acting from the absence of a false belief. In both cases Douglas is acting out of ignorance. Douglas did think about moral issues and considered the relevant factors and didn't intentionally commit a mistake in reasoning. Therefore ignorance of Douglas is not one arising out of negligence and hence he is not culpable for this ignorance. As regards the question of culpability of the act, Guerrero finds that it is natural to think that Douglas is culpable for killing the pig. On the basis of the above example, Guerrero shows the act is culpable even if it is out of blameless ignorance. I would object to this argument of Guerrero. I would suggest the following manner in which the example is to be given. In the first step, I would suggest the following two premises.

Douglas contemplates killing and eating a pig for dinner.

Douglas is uncertain whether it is morally wrong to kill a living animal.

If this is analyzed applying the theory of performing epistemic obligations, it is not at all difficult to conclude that killing a living organism is wrong. It appears that instead of putting the first premise as above Guerrero very conveniently placed it in such a manner where Douglas is contemplating about the moral status of a pig. I would argue that this way of placing the example of Guerrero is misleading. If the first step is given as I suggested above we find no difficulty to move towards the second one. In the second step, we will have to agree that a reasonable effort by Douglas will give him the right answer and he will not be left in uncertainty. The second step will then be followed to hold that Douglas is culpable for his ignorance. The above argument given by me will show that the argument of Guerrero is out of context. Guerrero's argument that even in cases where non culpable ignorance is present the act may be culpable is not on sound footing in the light of my above explanation. Guerrero further provides the principle Don't Know Don't Kill (hereinafter referred to as DKDK). Guerrero explains the principle of DKDK as follows.

"If someone knows that she doesn't know whether a living organism has significant moral status or not it is morally blameworthy for her to kill that organism or to have it killed unless she believes that there is something of substantial significance compelling her to do so" (Guerrero, 2007,p.79).

Guerrero declares and claims that it is his view that one does something for which one is culpable, morally blameworthy, when one kills a living organism and violates DKDK (Guerrero, 2007, p.79). I will put the above view of Guerrero in a simpler way i.e. it is morally wrong to kill any living organism.

The claim made by Guerrero that the above view is his own is not correct according to me. It appears that Guerrero declares as if DKDK is a novel principle found out by him. I refute the claim of Guerrero on the following reasons. In BC 599-527 Mahavira, the founder of Jainism has come forward with the theory of moral wrongness in killing any living organism. The principle of non violence is more comprehensive in the philosophical thoughts of Jainism. Killing of living organisms including minute creatures in the world were considered as morally wrong by the believers of Jainism. The followers of Jainism which is in existence in Asia often put a piece of cloth around the nose to prevent even a minute living creature being killed by man's inhalation and exhalation. Guerrero has discussed at length to find a way out on the moral status of other living organisms once you hold that killing a pig is wrong. According to me, such discussions are made for want of knowledge in the area of eastern philosophy and more specifically philosophy of Buddhism and Jainism. To kill any living organism is considered morally wrong and is an established principle way back in BC 527.

It appears that Guerrero has premeditated that an agent who does a bad act is held responsible even if the act is one out of morally blameless ignorance. Throughout the argument of Guerrero we find attempts made by him to show that a bad act is always culpable whether or not arising from blameless moral ignorance. I will argue that none of the examples given by Guerrero gives any credible challenge to the theory put forward by Rosen. Guerrero appears to link culpability and ignorance to the area of crime and punishment. He has focused on enforcement of law and punishment of the culprits who do a bad act. According to me, moral sanction or holding someone culpable for a bad act stands far removed from the legal spectrum and the punishments thereon.

Rosen explains the above referring to the example of Henry who refuses to pay his taxes in order to protest an unjust war. Henry believed that moral considerations in favour of protest are stronger than the legal reasons that support compliance. Henry may be punished under law, but he thinks that it is a price he his willing to pay. The blame is what an agent gets when he breaks the moral rule and not a violation of law (Rosen, 2003, p.80-81). I think I have given sufficient explanation with cogent reasons to show that Guerrero has miserably failed in his attempt to raise objections against the theories put forward by Rosen. The objection raised by Guerrero does not shake the foundation of Rosen's theory.

Holly Smith has stated the following on objective wrongness of an action and the agent's blameworthiness.

"No matter how terrible the act may be from an objective point of view, the agent is not blameworthy if he had an excuse for what he did" (Smith.H, 1983).

The view of Holly Smith seems to be over stretched. It implies that any action is justified if the agent has an excuse for the same. The blameworthiness of the act is not seen considered by Holly Smith applying the principles of epistemic obligation. Justification by excuse is also possible for a bad act even though it is a culpable one. Mere excuse for an action will not be a justification if it is arising out of culpable ignorance. Hence the blameworthiness of an act cannot be traced on the objective wrongness alone unless we are definite about the non-akratic nature of the act. Rosen on the other hand explains that whenever a person acts badly out of ignorance, Hence the blameworthiness of an act cannot be traced on the objective wrongness alone unless we are definite about the non-akratic nature of the act. Rosen on the other hand explains that whenever a person acts badly out of ignorance, the question will always be whether he has discharged the 'epistemic obligations'?

According to J. Wallace, it is unfair to blame someone for doing something if you are morally entitled to do it. It is unfair to blame someone for an act, if at the time of carrying out the act (blamelessly) lacked the general capacity to appreciate. He consequently was unable to act on the moral reasons for doing otherwise. According to Wallace, these principles explain the standard justifications and excuses. As rightly pointed out by Rosen, these norms do not cover cases of the ancient slave holder or the similar examples referred to in chapter 3. Diminished capabilities can also be a reason for blameless moral ignorance. An agent contracted with a virus which acts on the brain and if its effects are unpredictable it will be unfair on our part to hold him responsible or culpable for a bad act.

Uncertainty about attributions of moral responsibility can be found on the metaphysical claims regarding the impossibility of a free agency in a deterministic universe and that it encompasses all cases of moral responsibility, good and bad judgments of blame worthiness. Peter Strawson has made a successful attempt to reconcile between the deterministic approach (which he calls pessimistic) and non-deterministic approach (which he calls optimistic approach) in the matter of attributing moral responsibility. The pessimist claims determinism is true. It holds that the behaviour of an agent is also determined, and hence moral responsibility cannot be attributed to them. Strawson cites the example of punishing a child. Any bad act of a child is equally punishable or culpable. If the pessimist view (determinist view) is accepted in toto, then it does not make any difference whether it is a child or an adult. The truth of determinism does not thus shake the foundation of the concept of moral responsibility (Strawson in Watson 1982). Thus the culpability of an act with reference to Clear-eyed Akrasia becomes all the more convincing.

The importance that we attach to the attitudes and intentions of other human beings towards us is pointed out by Strawson. He also points to the extent to which our personal feelings and reactions depended upon or involve our beliefs about these attitudes and intentions. Considering occasions of resentment, Strawson refers to expressions such as 'he didn't mean to', 'he didn't realize', 'he didn't know', 'he couldn't help it', it was the only way', 'he was pushed', 'he had to do it' and so on. In all these cases, the offended person is normally expected to feel resentment. Strawson invites us to these common place examples (Strawson in Watson 1982). He shows that at times the agent responsible for the act is not fully responsible. Applying the argument of Rosen, in all the above examples experience of guilt is apparent. There is good evidence for the presence of Clear eyed Akrasia. The agent is blameworthy and culpable for his act.

Though objections are raised against the theories of Rosen on culpability and ignorance, I think I have given satisfactory explanation with cogent reasons against each of the objections. Against the objections raised by Fitzpatrick, I think I have answered with clarity that the objections raised by Fitzpatrick do not shake the foundation of the theories put forward by Rosen. The objection of Fitzpatrick that it is difficult to trace an episode of Clear-eyed Akrasia in the causal history of an act is proved to be incorrect on my explanation with examples. I have also given reasonable explanation to show why the objection raised by Guerrero is not acceptable. I have also referred to the views of Holly Smith, J. Wallace and Strawson, and have given sufficient explanation. Thus the theories of Rosen holds good even in the midst of objections raised against his views.

CHAPTER 5

BLAMELESS MORAL IGNORANCE AND RELIGIOUS BELIEF

IN THIS CHAPTER, I will deliberate in brief about the possibility of blameless moral ignorance arising out of religious belief. The example of Zacarias Moussaoui as explained in the opening paragraph of the introduction and similar such cases are discussed at length. I have built my case from this platform that an act out of blameless moral ignorance can also arise out of religious belief and/or misguided indoctrination.

Religion is founded on strong beliefs for which man is prepared to undertake great ordeals. The realization that logic and reasoning have limitations when it comes to explaining the ultimate reality can be said to be the foundation of religion. The concept of the Trinity in Christianity i.e. The Father, The Son and The Holy Spirit are seen as the base foundation. The followers are taught to have faith in the belief and to believe in the same. Thus Christianity is founded on an unquestionable faith in the belief of the existence of the Father, the Son and the Holy Spirit. Similarly, in the Islamic religion, the holy Quran and the scriptures thereon is treated as ultimate. The members of the religion are to follow the holy Quran and live according to Quran and the scriptures. The probability of brainwashing and indoctrination is very high in the realm of religious teachings by the religious fanatics or fundamentalists.

Now I would propose the following argument in support of the existence of blameless moral ignorance in a bad act arising out of religious belief.

X is born in an orthodox religious family and educated in an environment where religious faith is deep rooted. He does not get an opportunity to explore the metaphysical outlook of other religions. He has little exposure to philosophical thoughts. X is taught to believe that it is his duty to fight anybody who acts against his religious faith. Martyrdom in the course of such action is rewarded in the other world with eternal life. Consider a case where X does a bad act believing it to be right from his religious beliefs, and in the name of God. Can he be blamed? Is it not an act arising out of blameless moral ignorance? X is acting out of ignorance and that ignorance is not the outcome of thoughtlessness or carelessness or deliberate misconduct in the management of his opinion. There is no evidence of Clear-eyed Akrasia. Is it not a case falling under an act of blameless moral ignorance? I would say yes and the agent is not culpable for the act.

The above discussions are made only to make a platform to understand the possibility of indoctrination on religious belief. Now let us take a true example of Abu Hamsa, an Islamic fundamentalist, who manipulated a large number of youngsters by creating skewed religious beliefs. He enticed them with the reward in the other world and eternal life after death by dying in the name of Allah, through his powerful sermons at Finsbury Park, North London. To quote from his sermons: "We are all under the feet and heavy boots of the 'Kuffar' (unbeliever)" (Neill, S.O. and McGrory, D, 2006, p.21). "The 'intifida' started in Yemen when the people revolted and do you know why it started in Yemen? Because the prophet predicted a rise of the Aden army from Yemen" (Neill, S.O. and McGrory, D, 2006, p.155). In his sermon he also highlighted the reward of eternal life with 72 huries (virgin girls) in heaven. In the event of death in the holy war or Jihad in the name of God, an agent who does a bad act on the indoctrination of the above type can he be blamed for his act? Applying the principles for blameless moral ignorance as given by Rosen, it could be seen that the act of the agent is not an outcome of thoughtlessness. It is not negligence or deliberate misconduct in the management of the agent's own opinion. On the other hand, the agent is acting out of his own conviction. For example, Zacarias Moussaoui (the case referred to in the opening paragraph of the introduction), a suicide terrorist who participated in the 9/11 suicide mission in the United States. All other members of the suicide attack killed themselves in the mission. Zacarias Moussaoui is the only one caught alive. On an enquiry into the causal history of his act it is revealed that he was an ordinary man indoctrinated by Abu Hamsa (now in prison), an Islamic fundamentalist. The indoctrination was by way of powerful sermons on Jihad motivating the agent to act on the sermons. The sermons of Abu Hamsa were so powerful that it is quite natural that an ordinary prudent man may tend to believe his preachings. The indoctrination of Abu Hamsa at the Finsbury Park Mosque, North London, appears to have influenced Zacarias Moussaoui upon which he volunteered to become a suicide terrorist and participated in the 9/11 suicide attack. Zacarias Moussoui believed the teachings of Abu Hamsa as a true religious one and acted on the firm moral conviction that he is acting on the command of God and in the name of God. The act is only for renunciation and for eternal life. When Zacarias Moussaoui was brought for trial he said, "You missed an opportunity here to find out why people like me and Mohammed Atta (who led the 9/11 mission) have so much hatred". Further he said, "God curse America" (Neill, S.O. and McGrory, D, 2006, p.223). Now let us examine whether Zacarias Moussaoui is culpable for the act. The statement by him when brought for trial reveals that he is acting on behalf of God out of religious belief. He believed his action to be a right one. He does not experience any guilt or resentment. The causal history of his act does not reveal an event of thoughtlessness or carelessness or deliberate misconduct in the management of his opinion. The act is out of indoctrination. The ignorance caused thereon cannot be attributed to him. The ignorance is not culpable and consequently the act out of that ignorance is equally not culpable. There is no feeling of guilt or shame for the agent. The act of the agent is nothing but a non-akratic act and hence not culpable. Thus it is plausible that a bad act out of religious belief could be an act out of moral ignorance and hence not culpable.

There is similar indoctrination on religious belief as seen from the quotation below.

"What people in the west simply don't understand is that we love death more than they love life. It is my biggest regret that I have not been martyred yet, for this life is rotten. Osama Bin Laden, Nov 1996" (Abdel Bari Atwan, 2006, p. 89).

He goes on to say,

"The suicide mission is not only a physical event; it has an enormous psychological and ideological impact" (Abdel Bari Atwan, 2006, p. 90).

The suicide bomber being deployed, be it him or her, is a very powerful weapon, as he/she demonstrates the willingness to die for a cause. The logic of social psychology infers that such a cause might, at the very best be just. As a matter of fact there is evidence of abuse of religion to promote indoctrination on religious belief from the beginning of Islam and Christianity. Marco Polo's travelogues covering this aspect have been brought out succinctly by Colin Wilson, in his book "Criminal History of Mankind". Colin Wilson also describes the indoctrination on religious belief by the Popes in the medieval times.

CHAPTER 6

Possible Reasons for Blameless Moral Ignorance

In this chapter, I will analyze the possible reasons for blameless moral ignorance. Fighting for the motherland against foreign invasion or occupation is possibly the single major cause. Events arising out of social and cultural restrictions and pressures form another major reason. Forceful inducement of drugs, mistaken verdict, social injustice etc forms the third cause. Brainwash and indoctrination on religious belief, and blameless ignorance out of false belief form another major cause.

As we have discussed in chapter three, Rosen cites the example of the slave holder to establish the existence of blameless moral ignorance. The intellectual and cultural resources available in the period of the slave holder were tempered by the times they lived in. From the perspective of the times, it is difficult to find the practice of owning slaves to be wrong. To think otherwise the slave holder has to be a moral genius. Here the intellectual and cultural resources that existed seem to be the reason for blameless moral ignorance. Similarly in the case of Smith who gave differential treatment to his daughters as against his sons. Smith was doing what seemed reasonable to him. Tempered by the consideration of what he can plausibly be expected to have known at the relevant time. Here we can find the reason for blameless moral ignorance as the lack of knowledge which was not available at the relevant time and hence Smith cannot be blamed for not acquiring the same. According to Rosen, one of the lessons of history is that the transformation of a moral sensibility is a monumental task (Rosen, 2003, p.67).

The inducement of drugs forcefully can also be a reason for blameless moral ignorance as the agent loses the capacity for self control and results in an aggressive action. Mistaken verdict after an honest review of the considerations can also be an act out of blameless moral ignorance. Rosen gives an example of Truman issuing the order to bomb Hiroshima. Assume that Truman was given all the necessary inputs and details by his advisors and after weighing all the circumstances and inputs Truman decides to order bombing in Hiroshima. The decision according to Truman is right and he believed the action to be right. Can he be blamed for the act though it is considered as monumentally wrong? According to Rosen, Truman is not to be blamed as the decision taken is after considering all the relevant facts and circumstances and at the best he might have gone wrong about how to weigh competing demands. The act is not one against his own better judgment but on the other hand he has acted in tune with his better judgment. Of course we have the wisdom of hindsight with us, a luxury that was not available to him in the thick of war (Rosen, 2003, p.69-70).

Brainwash and indoctrination is another area where blameless ignorance becomes a possibility. It is plausible that an agent X is brainwashed by Y and the indoctrination is such that the agent believes in the teachings of Y as truth and act out of the same. The agent never feels guilt nor is he shameful of his act. There is no Clear-eyed Akrasia. The agent is not acting against his better judgment. The act comes within the arena of blameless moral ignorance and hence not culpable. The existence of blameless moral ignorance exonerates the agent from moral responsibility. Rosen relies on the existence of Akrasia in the causal history of an act to hold the agent responsible or culpable for the act. According to Rosen, an akratic agent is not acting out of ignorance. He knows that morally righteous would be to do 'A'. His moral reasons are compelling, and all things considered A is the right thing to do. He still can't bring himself to do A and does something else. In this case the act is not from ignorance and is not to be excused (Rosen, 2003, p.83). Here Rosen refers to a considered judgment, which is Clear-eyed Akrasia i.e. acting against one's considered judgment about what there is most reason for him to do. In the case of the ancient slave holder, if we are to ask him, he will definitely say that he does not feel guilty or shame in holding slaves. In those days it was a part of the value system, and the landed gentry used to pride on the number of slaves they owned. Applying the principles laid down by Rosen for blameless factual ignorance, the act of the slave holder is nothing but blameless moral ignorance and he is not culpable for the act.

Fighting for the motherland as a part of the war, one decides to become a suicide bomber to destroy the enemy or the invader. Can he be blamed for the act? In the Second World War, Japanese pilots defending the homeland against an invading American Navy crashed their fighter planes deliberately into the enemy ships killing themselves and destroying the enemy. A suicide fighter pilot is considered as the divine wind or Kamikaze and is respected as a patriotic person than being blamed for the act.

The suggestion that the agent could or may have known may not work out for blame. A better approach would be to establish whether the agent is blameless for not knowing as pointed out by Rosen. The available social circumstances under which an agent is brought up can also be a reason for an act out of blameless moral ignorance. Will it be fair if we attribute moral responsibility to an agent who by himself is not responsible for not knowing certain things irrespective of the best efforts? Can the agent be blamed for his ignorance? I would say no because he is blameless for not knowing as it is not because of his negligence. Bad upbringing can also be a reason for holding an agent not culpable for a bad act if it is a result of his bad upbringing. The agent does not have control on his bad upbringing and is not to be blamed for the same.

A false belief can also sometimes be a reason for a non culpable act. For example, among the Sikh community (a community which believes in the Sikh religion in India) when a child is born he is imposed with religious beliefs. The child is taken to their religious temple and is insisted to vow certain beliefs as a part of their religious belief. One among such belief imposed is that he or she shall not have sexual intercourse with the member of a Muslim community ever in their life time. The belief is further sharpened in the child's mind by taking the child to the art gallery of their religion and showing the painted pictures describing or narrating the atrocities meted out by them from the Muslim community which include mass raping, looting, killing and so on. Any member of the Sikh community who violates the above said vow is ostracized from the family and the community, and is blamed for the act. A Sikh community member marrying a Muslim is discriminated by the community, can they be blamed? I would prefer to argue that their act is out of blameless moral ignorance. As it is arising out of a religious belief or false belief and is not an outcome of thoughtlessness or carelessness and there is no evidence of Clear-eyed Akrasia and the act is a non akratic one. Thus the possible reasons for blameless moral ignorance are numerous and are exhaustive.

CHAPTER 7

Suicide Terrorism and Blameless Moral Ignorance

In this chapter, I will discuss suicide terrorism and blameless moral ignorance. I have referred to the findings of Robert A. Pape in his book 'Dying to Win'. He conducted factual research on 462 cases of suicide terrorists during the period 1980-2004. I have formulated my argument that suicide terrorists are acting out of blameless (moral or factual) ignorance and hence are not culpable for the act. My argument is on the ground that suicide terrorists are either acting on religious indoctrination or on a patriotism-based act of dying for the country or a combination of both. In all these cases the suicide terrorist is acting out of blameless moral ignorance. It is unfair to blame them and I argue that they are not culpable for the act.

Suicide terrorism is witnessed by the world as the most powerful, destructive and horrifying method of self destruction and the murder of random innocents. Robert A. Pape finds that suicide terrorism is mainly a response to foreign occupation and Islamic fundamentalism is not closely associated with suicide terrorism as many people think. According to Borowilz, self is the main motivation for suicide terrorism. Ken Wilber describes terrorism on the basis of his theory known as AQ AL (All Quadrants All Levels). Wilber uses them as representing the society. He further states that all must be attended equally in order to prevent pathological personalities in the society from developing. Marcuse in his book 'One Dimensional Man' favours suicide as a glorified act. The mindset theory holds that not only are suicide terrorists suffering from broken self development but also the society or the culture breeding them is suffering from a similar problem.

An analysis of the datas of suicide terrorists from 1980-2004 by Robert A. Pape on 462 suicide missions killing themselves reveal that most of them are walk in volunteers and only very few are criminals and long time members of the terrorists group. It is alarming that for most of the suicide terrorists, their first experience with violence is their own suicide mission. Against the occupier theory of Robert A. Pape, critics pointed out that when there is religious difference between the occupier and the occupant, it enables the terrorist leaders to demonize the occupier in vicious ways. According to Daniel Bell, lack of a philosophical outlook on global economy, culture clashes, mass immigration, how to end the human suffering, how to guard against the totalitarians etc also paved the way for the end of ideology.

An analysis of the history, much of the war and terrorism can be seen as a war on ideology. But the present day suicide terrorism reflects the end of ideology. Is the group dynamics that drives the individual to successfully complete his/her mission by hitting the target killing themselves? Suicide bombers are seen not united by race, religion, classes, intelligence, economics or education. They come in all hues and shapes, such as from the rich background and from the poor, well educated and the illiterates, intelligent ones and even moronic ones, religious fundamentalists and non religious. In most of the cases suicide bombers are found to be average and absolutely normal.

Abu Hamsa an Islamic fundamentalist as already referred to in chapter four, has manipulated large number of youngsters by indoctrination and interpreting the teachings of Islam in a skewed manner so that agents voluntarily walk in to become suicide terrorists. The suicide terrorist who participated in the 9/11 suicide mission in the United States are found to be the victims of indoctrination of Abu Hamsa. The indoctrination is such that they believed the teachings of Abu Hamsa and turned out to be suicide terrorists.

I wish to proceed on the culpability of the suicide terrorist and to locate whether their act is an act out of blameless moral ignorance. The leaders behind creating suicide terrorists may have different objectives, motivation and ulterior intentions which can be for political gain, for coercing the occupier to move out from the territory and so on. This forms the larger spectrum of the effects of a suicide terrorist's attack. I am keen only on the area of the question of the culpability of the act of suicide terrorists. I proceed on the view that suicide terrorists are not culpable. Their act is one out of ignorance and the ignorance is not an outcome of thoughtlessness or carelessness or deliberate misconduct in the management of their opinion. They are not acting against their own better judgment and their act is one out of blameless moral ignorance and they are not culpable.

I would prefer to give a few examples to demonstrate the possibility of a suicide terrorist being not culpable. LTTE (Liberation Tigers Tamil Eelam) suicide bombers are motivated to become suicide bombers as a part of their fight for their motherland. They are motivated by their political and social environment as well as the indoctrination carried out by the organization. They are driven by the indoctrination on ethnic nationalism and the LTTE suicide bomber takes it as a privilege to die for a cause which is the dream of their motherland (Rohan Gunaratna, 2000). I would argue that an LTTE suicide bomber is standing at par with a Kamikaze of Japan in the Second World War and their act is not an akratic one as they are not acting against their better judgment. On the other hand, they act in tune with their better judgment and hence those suicide terrorists should be considered as acting out of blameless moral ignorance and are not culpable for the act.

Afghanistan's child bombers are another example of suicide terrorist's act out of coercion. The Taliban group using force takes young children from the residence of the villagers and they are indoctrinated on skewed belief and are prepared by the organization as suicide bombers. It is hard to find an episode of Clear-eyed Akrasia in this kind of a suicide terrorist and he is definitely acting out of blameless moral ignorance (Glyn Williams, 2007).

What I am trying to explain is not about suicide terrorism being used as a weapon, but the blameworthiness of the act as a suicide terrorist. The suicide terrorist can either belong to the category of those who are indoctrinated on a belief (religious or otherwise) or those who are fighting for their motherland risking their lives. Both the categories cannot be blamed as they are acting out of blameless moral ignorance and hence not culpable. Thus I would argue that suicide terrorists are not culpable. There is no episode of Clear-eyed Akrasia in the causal history of suicide terrorists in the above referred examples and I argue that this principle apply for the generality in the case of suicide terrorists. Thus I would argue that it is plausible that suicide terrorists are acting out of blameless moral ignorance and hence not culpable.

CHAPTER 8

CONCLUSION

I N MY DISCUSSIONS in chapter three, I have elaborated on culpability and ignorance. I have put forward enough examples in support of the theory of blameless moral ignorance as given by Rosen. I think I have established beyond doubt the existence of blameless moral ignorance. In chapter four, I have considered in detail the various objections raised against the theory of blameless moral ignorance and the parity thesis of Rosen i.e. whenever an agent acts from ignorance whether factual or moral, he is culpable of the act only if he is culpable for the ignorance from which he acts. I believe that I have given significant arguments against all the objections raised against Rosen's theory and why it holds well.

In chapter five, I have argued that an act out of a religious belief can also be an act out of moral ignorance, and in such cases also it will be unfair to hold the agent culpable. I have also argued and established the possibility of indoctrination and brainwashing on religious belief. I have also given a true example of a suicide terrorist who participated in the 9/11 attack, in support of my argument. Even a brutal act out of a religious belief can also be one out of blameless moral ignorance and the agent is not culpable for the act.

In chapter six, I have explained possible reasons for blameless moral ignorance and I think that I have successfully explained the reasons for blameless moral ignorance. Fighting for the motherland and occupying forces, forcefully induced drugs, mistaken verdict, brainwashing and indoctrination on religious belief, and blameless ignorance out of false belief form major causes.

From chapter three to chapter six, I have developed my arguments in support of the existence of blameless moral ignorance and the plausibility of suicide terrorists being not culpable for their act. In the final chapter, I have presented my case that suicide terrorists are not culpable as they act out of blameless moral ignorance. There are cases of indoctrination of religious belief and moral ignorance which cause a suicide terrorist act. Cases of suicide bombers acting out of coercion also exist. Manipulation or indoctrination in the name of the motherland or a group or cult is also evident in suicide terrorism. I have argued that most of the cases in which suicide terrorists act are one of the above or a combination of the categories I have mentioned in chapter five and six.

Based on the above, I have arrived at the following conclusions:

(a) Blameless (moral or factual) ignorance is a possibility.

(b) Parity thesis of Rosen that whenever an agent acts from ignorance, whether factual or moral, he is culpable for the act only if he is culpable for the ignorance from which he acts, proves to be true and apply to all cases.

(c) The theory of blameless moral ignorance and non culpability of a bad act out of blameless moral ignorance is equally applicable to all cases in general irrespective of how cruel or brutal the act is.

(d) It is plausible that most of the suicide terrorists act out of blameless (moral or factual) ignorance.

(e) All suicide terrorists acting out of blameless (moral or factual) ignorance are not culpable and it will be unfair to blame them.

(f) An act out of blameless moral ignorance can also arise out of religious belief and/or misguided indoctrination.

(g) It proves that it is unfair to blame or hold one culpable for an act out of blameless (moral or factual) ignorance.

I have started my argument to hold that it is plausible that an agent is not culpable for an act which is brutal from the objective point of view. A suicide terrorist act is brutal and it often results in the killing of a large number of innocents. It is at times unthinkable even to bear the thought of such acts being non culpable. This of course is when we look at the objective wrongness of the act. It is not my intention to vindicate suicide terrorists and exonerate them from legal liability or punishment thereon.

There is the question of attributing moral responsibility to an agent who acts as a suicide bomber or has participated in a suicide mission. What has provoked my thought is that in a large number of reported cases of suicide terrorism, the agents are all found to be normal individuals having no criminal background. A study conducted by Robert A. Pape in his book 'Dying to Win' about 462 actual cases, also revealed to me that suicide terrorism is footed on a different plane. It is alarming that most of the suicide terrorists are walk-in volunteers and they come from all walks of life and all strata of society. So the question of attributing moral responsibility on suicide terrorists has become all the more relevant.

I will add that the human mind is both complex and powerful; it is a difficult task to definitely identify an episode of Clear-eyed Akrasia in the causal history of an act.

There is always the risk of going wrong while we hold someone culpable for a bad act if we merely refer to the objective wrongness of the act alone. This is an area where I feel we require further research and as much in detail.

I agree with and accept the statement of Rosen that God or a super psychologist alone can confidently identify an episode of Clear-eyed Akrasia in the causal history of an act.

CHAPTER 9

The Way Ahead

Philosophy as a Compulsory Subject in the Educational Curriculum to Prevent Suicide Terrorism

T HE FINDINGS IN the previous chapter show that the majority of the suicide terrorists fall in the category of those arising out of indoctrination or brainwash. According to Bakken, the indoctrination into the terrorist organization is done so primarily through training exercises. Training can last up to several months, depending on intricateness, complexity and urgency of the operation. Religious indoctrination as well as anti propaganda towards the targeted objective is subjected to the potential suicide bomber on a regular basis. These individuals attend classes where emphasis is placed on those parts of Quran and Hadith that glorify martyrdom and the benefits of after life. The students are required to show their commitment to the group by completing assigned tasks that test the recruit's ability to follow orders and manage secrecy.

It is important to note that the modus operandi of the terrorist organizations is not the area which I wish to emphasize. I am more on the question of the surprising number of walk-in volunteers who join the terrorist organization. The indoctrination or brainwash, be it religious or otherwise, which entices or attracts walk-in volunteers is to be viewed seriously. Why does a well educated person, with no criminal background, become a walk-in volunteer?

According to McDermott, "most of the men of September 11 came from apolitical and unexceptional backgrounds. They evolved into devout, pious young men who, over time, drew deeper and deeper into Islam. As they did, they debated endlessly how best to serve their God, how to fulfill what they came to regard as sacred obligations. They saw themselves as soldiers of God, which prompts the obvious question: what kind of religious belief could empower men to inflict such great harm and deprivation on other men, women and children?"

Let us examine the case of Mohammad Atta. He led the September 11 attack in the United States and killed himself along with thousands of innocents. Mohammad Atta Al Sayyid was born on 1st September 1968 in Kafr el sheikh, in Egypt. His initial ages were in a suburb of Cairo. Atta received a degree in Architecture from the Cairo University and a Degree in Urban Planning from the Technical University of Hamburg in Germany. During his time in Germany, the fellow students recalled his anti American views. Mohammad Atta was found increasingly religious and joined an Islamic prayer group at the University. Thereafter, he joined Al-Quaida and led the September 11 attack. A discerning view after the analysis of the background of Mohammad Atta is that in all likelihood he was under religious indoctrination. The containment of skewed religious indoctrination is a major challenge for one and all across the world. A perusal of the academic background of Mohammad Atta would indicate that in the schools he would have studied typical subjects relating to science, social science, maths and language. After the basic education, Atta has specialized into the branch of Architecture engineering. Throughout his educational curriculum, apparently, he has not had an opportunity to study philosophy as a subject. It is more so since the said subject is not part of the educational curriculum.

Any perspective on suicide terrorism would be incomplete without LTTE. They streamlined and institutionalized the modern day suicide terrorism. In LTTE, glorification of death for the cause goes hand in hand with training. Black Tigers, the suicide terrorist squad of LTTE included Hindus and Christians. They were picked from young volunteers. Many of them have been exposed to the ravages of war in their formative years. They were separated from their families and brought up in the LTTE ambience for a number of years. There was an organized indoctrination of their minds by glorifying self-sacrifice as the highest form of service to the Tamil nation. In the context of suicide bombers, LTTE does not use the Tamil word "tharkkolai" (suicide) but refers it as "tharkkodai" (gift of self). This is not merely a semantic exercise; it indicates their mindset in sacrificing own life as a gift for the cause. It was Dhanu, a woman cadre who carried out the attack on Rajiv Gandhi, the then Prime Minister of India on May 21, 1991. Thenmozhi Rajaratnam (believed to be the real name of Dhanu), who was a Tamil Christian from Srilanka, was selected, indoctrinated and trained by LTTE. The power of training and indoctrination was evident by the way the execution was carried out. The limited information available on the suicide terrorist indicates that she has had traditional education. Needless to say that apparently she has not had the benefit of exposure to philosophy in her schooling.

It is my intention to focus on the introduction of philosophy in school curriculum to develop critical thinking ability of the mind. The concept needs to be put in perspective. Schools need to train and prepare students to think for themselves more ably. The study of philosophy would train students to ask questions like "What is man?" Why are there so many varying theories about him? What is free will? Is there a meaning to life? Does the universe exist? Is there a life after death? Is suffering in the world avoidable? Why do the beliefs of men vary so much from people to people? Is there something called absolute truth? Is it possible for us to know if we have found truth? Studying philosophy in school could give a perspective on how these questions were answered at various points of time in history. How the arguments for and against have changed over the times. The student understands and learns to analyze the outline of any specific question. In addition, he also gets to explore the fabric of critical thought itself. A student so educated would be able to take apart and reject faulty arguments. Thus gain the critical ability on how to think. Critical thinking is to be groomed from school days; to prevent the vulnerability of being brainwashed to accepting ideas at face value. Philosophy would enable the students to be open-minded and to enable their minds to think for it.

Ancient history of both the East and the West shows that philosophy as a subject was always an integral part of the educational curriculum. Each subject was taught with reference to its relation to philosophy as well. The word Philosophy is derived from Greek meaning a rational investigation of the truths and principles of being, knowledge or conduct. The branches in philosophy include Natural philosophy, Moral philosophy and Metaphysical philosophy. In general, the subject philosophy can be classified as Eastern and Western. The Western philosophy traces its origin in Greece and is more or less considered as

Greek philosophy. Greek philosophy begins with an inquiry into the essence of the objective world. From the external nature it gradually turns its eye inward on man himself. Shifting of interest from nature to man leads to the study of the human mind. It includes human conduct of logic, ethics, psychology, politics and poetics. Of these special attention is on ethics at the school stage. The chief question for philosophy now becomes what is the highest good, what is the end and aim of life. In this investigative journey, the study of metaphysics and of human knowledge becomes indispensable. Consequently the issue of God and man's relation to God that is central to the theological approach comes to the forefront.

The second phase of the development of Western philosophy is the period of Sophists and Socrates. That 'truth' may be reached by the employment of a logical method was the golden contribution of Socrates. This paved way for the science of ethics by defining the meaning of the 'good'. Following Socrates, Plato and Aristotle laid foundations to the rational theories of knowledge (i.e. logic) and theories on conduct (i.e. ethics) and theories of states (Politics). They worked out a comprehensive system for metaphysics i.e. the speculative thoughts. Plato and Aristotle were followed by many famous philosophers including Pythagoras, Heraclites, John Locke, George Berkeley, David Hume and Leibniz and so on. All these philosophers contributed to Western philosophy which helped the development of the nation, the individual and the society. We can find the traces of the influence of philosophy at all points of time in history.

Understanding of the subject philosophy and its branches help individuals to streamline their thoughts to achieve the highest good. Existentialism holds a very popular position in the contemporary philosophy. Existentialism emerged in its current form in Paris following World War II. It has become one of the major current thoughts in Germany with Martin Heidegger and Jaspers among its leaders. Soren Kierkegaard laid down the main themes of this philosophy in the 19th century. All these philosophers had in common the issue about existence, human existence, and the conditional quality of the existence of human individuals. According to the existentialist philosophers, the individual had over the centuries been pushed into the backgrounds by systems of thoughts, historical events and technological forces. The major system of philosophy had rarely paid attention to the personal concerns of the individuals. Philosophy for the most part dealt with the technical problems of metaphysics, ethics and theory of knowledge in general. According to them, materialism, determinism and absolute idealism threatened to engulf the free individuals. Thus we could see that history always recognized the influence of philosophy as a subject in the main stream and has even changed the society as such which has been proven time and again. Studying philosophy as a part of the educational curriculum will definitely enlighten the individual on the thoughts of various philosophers including the contemporary philosophers and to understand and sharpen their thoughts.

Eastern philosophy is considered synonymous with Indian philosophy. The beginning of Indian philosophy takes us back more than thirty centuries. The earliest literature available is the Vedas. The Vedas and the Upanishads are considered to be directly and indirectly responsible for most of the philosophical speculations in Indian philosophy. It is important to note that Indian philosophy is not Hindu philosophy. Traditionally Indian philosophies are divided into two broad classes such as Orthodox and Heterodox. The first class of philosophical system composes of six major groups such as Mimamsa, Vedantha, Samkhya, Yoga, Naya and Vaisesika. These groups are regarded as Orthodox not because they believe in God but because they accept the authorities of the Vedas. Mimamsa and Samkhya do not believe in God as a creator of the world. Yet they are called Orthodox because they believe in the authoritativeness of the Vedas. Under the Heterodox system there are three schools such as Carvakas, the Buddhas and the Jainas. They are called Heterodox as they do not believe in the authority of the Vedas. Indian philosophy is essentially spiritual. The history of Indian thought illustrates the endless quest of the mind. Among these, the Carvakas school of philosophy is purely non-spiritual and they do not believe in the concept of life after death, law of Karma or the eternal moral order etc. They believe in the concept of materialism i.e. there is no life after death and that the human body is made up of the Pancha Bhuthas (i.e. air, water, fire, earth and Akasha (either). In Buddhism, ignorance is considered as the root cause for all evils and it emphasizes on the importance of meditation and the practical life for self control.

There is also a misconstrued perception that Indian philosophy is pessimist, dogmatic and is based on blind belief than being rational. Indian philosophy as well as the Western philosophy at length reflects the cultural effects on the individual. The west is influenced by Western philosophy and orients by Eastern philosophical thoughts. Over a period of time and more so from the nineteenth century, the study of philosophy as a subject has declined considerably. Philosophy has moved away from the central place it enjoyed in the academic scheme of things and sidelined. The handfuls of people who study philosophy become a privileged lot with the benefit of critical thinking. A privilege that is abused by vested interests to brainwash young minds which are vulnerable in the absence of critical thinking, a gift of philosophy. The importance of studying subject philosophy as a part of the educational curriculum becomes all the more relevant as it is a reflection of the history, culture and its effect on the society as such.

Now let us get back to Mohammad Atta. What was the mental disposition of Mohammad Atta prior to his becoming a suicide terrorist? What his mental state was is of importance. It is the mental state and disposition which creates the emotion and emotional response of the individual. Mental disposition are those mental habits that influence everything one does. These are the persisting modifications of the mind which underlie the sequence of the mental state. Examples for mental dispositions are beliefs and desires, knowledge, memories, abilities, powers, skills, habits, inhibitions, obsessions, phobias and virtues and vices. The mental states are different from mental dispositions and the examples for mental states are perceptions, sensations and pains, pangs of hunger or thirst, dreams and day dreams, moments of despair, boredom or lust, flashes of inspiration, recollections, thoughts and so on. It is my view that the emotional response of the individual would be more influential than indoctrination in the making of a suicide terrorist. The background of Mohammad Atta has shown his anti American bias prior to becoming a suicide terrorist. His belief or mental state and emotional bias has in all probabilities been well understood and exploited by his perpetrators. The indoctrination would have been programmed to this end to achieve a fiercely committed suicide terrorist. Mental dispositions and mental states interact in a number of ways. A mental state can initiate a mental disposition. According to the empiricist philosophers of the 17th and 18th centuries, the intentionality of a mental state is wholly constructed out of its subjectivity (R. Willheim, 1999) on the emotions of the originating conditions.

Theory of emotions also falls in the arena of philosophy. Emotions require determinate cognitive base such as perceptions, memories, anticipations and occurrence beliefs. The perception of the individual depends on the concepts and the knowledge available to the individual. In the case of Mohammed Atta it could be seen that, apparently, his knowledge or exposure to the field of philosophy is almost nil. Had he an opportunity to study philosophy during his educational curriculum, his perceptions would have been different as also his emotional response.

Let us take the case of Hani Saleh Hasan Hanjour, who hijacked the American airlines flight 77 crashing the plane into the Pentagon as part of the September 11 attacks. Born in Saudi Arabia, Hanjour first came to the United States in 1991, enrolled at the University of Arizona where he studied English for a few months and returned to Saudi Arabia and came back in 1996 for studying English in California, and by 1999 he studied lessons taking flying in Arizona and received his commercial pilot certificate. Hanjour returned to Saudi Arabia, to be a radical Islamic and apparently became a victim of religious indoctrination. That he became a suicide terrorist is history now. In both the cases, we find that they did not have any criminal background nor were they involved in any criminal activities prior to the September 11 attack. The first criminal act of the aforesaid two persons is the September 11 attack and they died in the action.

In both the cases, they have had good education in the conventional sense. But I would say the lack of exposure to the subject philosophy made them vulnerable to religious indoctrination and brainwash. They were easily carried away by the glib perspectives of the perpetrators or those with vested interests and ended up being suicide terrorists. Assume that Hanjour did get an opportunity to learn philosophy. This would have given him good exposure to the philosophical thinking of both eastern and western philosophers. Consequently he would have had a critical thinking mind and it would have been impossible for anyone to brainwash or misguide him with religious indoctrination. The only suicide terrorist who is still alive, who participated in the September 11 attack is Zacarias Moussaoui about whom we have discussed in the previous chapters. Even the said Zacarias Moussaoui does not have any feeling of guilt or remorse about the September 11 attack. The religious indoctrination is so powerful that it keeps the individuals removed from reality and they are made to believe that the existing world is nothing but an illusion. The indoctrination promotes the life after death laced with glory. It goes without saying that the introduction of philosophy in schools becomes all the more important under these circumstances to keep the mind on a sound footing.

Lets us consider the case of Dr. Kafeel Ahmed. He burnt to death in an attempted suicide terrorist attack at the Glasgow Airport,

Scotland, UK. This is yet another example in support of my above argument. Ahmed was born into a large, wealthy medical family in Bangalore, India. He studied mechanical engineering at a university before attending Queen's College in Belfast for Masters in aeronautical engineering between 2001 and 2003. From there he went to Cambridge to undertake a three-year doctorate at the Anglia Ruskin University. As a former president of the Islamic society while at the university in Belfast, Ahmed was deeply involved in political Islam. He also shared a home with members of the fundamentalist group Hizb ut-Tahir while living in Cambridge. Police in India also claimed that he and his brother Sabeel had links to the missionary sect Tablighi Jamaat. Information of records of online chats and e-mail did prove how he was manipulated by indoctrination. The carefully planned plot envisaged car bomb explosions which failed because of loose connection. The failure left Ahmed with no option but suicide. Kafeel Ahmed poured petrol over himself and lit fire. A month later, the Indian engineer died after suffering excruciating agony while being cared for in the hospital (Bird, 2008). Kafeel Ahmed was a well educated person. Indoctrination by vested interests made him a suicide terrorist. The education curriculum of India, especially at the schools, does not provide philosophy as a subject. Most of the children do not get any exposure to philosophy let alone opportunity for studying. Typically the present system of education in India caters to basic education at the school level. Thereafter each student selects a particular discipline for specialization or professional course. Even for the students who do well and attend professional courses, the word philosophy is steeped in mystique. They are vulnerable to the manipulative teachings of the radicals who cite skewed versions of philosophy. The exploiters also resort to exotic promises and convictions of glory in the life after death. To say the least the typical education does not equip the students with sufficient materials for grooming his thoughts against such manipulations. They are susceptible and easily brainwashed or indoctrinated, be it religious or otherwise.

The majority of the suicide terrorist can be grouped into two major categories. The educated elite, lacking the formal exposure to philosophy, who are vulnerable to the skewed perceptions and brainwashing of the perpetrators. The second category is those from the relatively marginalized section of the society where they have not had much opportunity for education of any kind. It is conclusive that brainwashing or religious indoctrination has been effective due to the lack of independent philosophical thinking capability of the suicide terrorists. What comes through is the need to develop the mind on sound thinking process which is best done through introduction of philosophy as a compulsory subject in the school education curriculum across the world. The time has come for this issue is to be addressed adequately at the grass root level to get rid of the malaise of suicide terrorism.

Let us consider the case of Dr. Aafia Siddiqui. She is an American-educated Pakistani cognitive_neuroscientist who was convicted after a jury trial in a U.S. Federal Court of assault with intent to murder her U.S. interrogators in Afghanistan. The charges carried a maximum sentence of life in prison. In September 2010, she was sentenced by the U.S. judge to 86 years in prison. Born in Karachi, Pakistan, on March 2, 1972, Aafia was one of three children of Mohammad Siddiqui, a doctor trained in England, and Ismet, a homemaker. Mohammed, Aafia's brother, is an architect living in Houston with his wife, a pediatrician, and their children. Fowzia, Aafia's sister, is a Harvard-trained neurologist who was working at the Sinai Hospital in Baltimore until she decided to go back to Pakistan.

Aafia Siddiqui moved to Texas in 1990 to be near her brother and had good enough grades after spending a year at the University of Houston to transfer to MIT. Siddiqui's fellow students say she was a quiet, studious woman who was devout in her religious beliefs but not a fundamentalist. She often wore a headscarf, for example, but didn't cover her face. While at MIT, Siddiqui apparently joined an association for Muslim students. She wrote three guides for members who wanted to teach others about Islam. Other references, however, reveal a passion for Islam that could be called hard line. It is here she is believed to have come across the terrorists. It is hard to believe that someone like her could have participated in activities to support terrorism. She is believed to have fired upon her US interrogators apparently without any concern for her life. It is definite that an exposure to philosophy in her schooling would have definitely prevented her from becoming an active promoter of suicide terrorism (Bone and Hussain, 2008).

Among the contemporary Indian Philosophers, Mohammed Iqbal (1876-1938) occupies a unique position. His contributions to Modern Islamic thought are mainly in the areas of theological method; doctrine of God; doctrine of man; change and social order; and political ideas. According to him, the general aim of his philosophical thinking is the reconstruction of religious thought in Islam. The Western philosophers who have influenced Mohammed Iqbal's thoughts include Burgson, Nietzsche and other British Idealists. The concept of 'God or Reality' according to Mohammed Iqbal is monism i.e. God is only one and is omnipotent (all powerful) and supremely good and the creator of the world. According to Mohammed Iqbal, the distinction between the 'God and Absolute' is irrelevant to Islam and he feels that the cosmological, ontological and teleological proofs for God's existence are attempts on the part of our limited intellect to comprehend the nature of God. Such proofs are utterly inadequate because they are based on superficial interpretation of experience and not on an intuitive experience of reality. He also criticized the cosmological argument and insisted that it is inconsistent with the causal law. Mohammed Iqbal claims that the Quran describes the source of knowledge—the one that can know reality directly as 'fuad' which means heart. Mohammed Iqbal claims that the heart is the faculty of intuition. The teachings of Indian philosophers like Mohammed Iqbal are alien to the present day education system in the absence of philosophy in curriculum.

According to Philip Cam, in his article *philosophy for a thinking curriculum*, "If we are serious about teaching children to think, then we need to be serious about structuring the curriculum around thinking. This requires us to pay attention to the general thinking strategies and broad conceptual understandings that find a natural home in philosophy. By looking to the concepts and procedures of philosophy, we can help to integrate the curriculum and at the same time make children more effective participants in the process of learning".

As a discipline the very focus of philosophy is on cognitive thinking. Philosophy is about analytical thinking and includes thoughts on thinking itself. Philosophical approach is centered on the process of thinking. Consequently philosophy has developed skill sets for searching deep for concepts and logic. Philosophy at the school level envisages teaching students on using of these skill sets. This would lay the bedrock of mental foundation that enables holistic approach and systematic approach to logic. These will enable children to effectively engage in their own development of intellect, the ultimate goal being able to think for them.

Plato said about the word of Socrates as follows:

"you will find his words first full of sense, as no other are, next most divine and containing the finest images of virtue, and reaching far these, in fact reaching to everything which it profits a man to study who is to become noble and good". A good example would be to look back at the ancient Greek times and how Socrates developed conversation based discussions to arrive at the real and objective meanings of simple concepts such as love, friendship, courage and virtue which are as applicable today as it was so many centuries ago. (Dr. Sharma).

In the present day world, the children and the adults are growing up in an environment of information overload. Even a discerning mind would find itself not so well equipped to deal with the diverse views and varying situations, to arrive at conclusions based on comprehension and understanding and to prioritize them. In the environment of fast paced changes and varying degrees of uncertainty, there is constant pressure on individuals to keep pace with the change or be left out. The society that we live in is also going through phases of change with its share of socio-cultural changes and complexities compounded with rising levels on intolerance. More than ever there is a need for children to develop the capability to think and have an open mind. The introduction of philosophy in schools would help improve the thinking quotient and the all important value system. Philosophy is the bedrock of the mind which will nurture and promote creative thinking and make the mind more discerning and sharp, a quality which needs to be inculcated and strengthened.

The education system has undergone considerable changes since the days of the industrial revolution. The advent of mechanization and machines have brought with it the engineering oriented education. The engineering based and oriented studies have developed to be more vertically specialized as also has the field of medicine. The advent of computers and the revolution in information and related technology have further made exponential growth in the knowledge domain. While the education has well addressed the requirements of technology from time to time, we have floundered in the holistic approach towards life and society which was an integral part of the education system. It goes without saying that holistic thinking skills and clear understanding of concepts is a pre-requisite to make connections between different academic disciplines. Philosophy would bring in that much needed flexibility and orientation in thinking to always strive for a holistic understanding of things.

The Gurukul system of education in ancient India was related to the quest of studies. Here the guru or the teacher lived with his family members along with his students and imparted education to them in varied fields. Gurukul was generally established in forests, away from the din and bustle of normal life. A shishya (student/disciple) served his guru for years and gained the faith of the guru with his determination, discipline, sincerity and intelligence before he was provided an opportunity to acquire the knowledge of different subjects. The concept was that the student lived with the guru or mentor who would impart all-round education. The guru would teach every subject with relevance to life and with the associated philosophy as well.

The ancient Greek education focused heavily on training the entire person, which included education of the mind, body, and imagination. The specific purposes of Greek education differed from state to state. The Spartans placed a high emphasis on military training, while the Athenians traditionally gave more attention to music, literature, dance, and later also to the natural sciences, such as biology and chemistry, as well as philosophy, rhetoric, and sophistry-the art of presenting an argument using deception and reason to persuade the public to agree with a certain point of view.

It goes without saying that any proficiency achieved without the sound back up of philosophy and the ethics, aesthetic, logic, metaphysics and related topics would be incomplete. Such education would not give the best for the society. A medical practitioner lacking ethics would be prone to the corporate greed promoted by MNCs (multi national companies) and may engage even in selling harmful drugs purely for monetary gains. In the process, human values and medical ethics get left by the wayside. This is equally applicable to the lawyer, the judge, the policeman, the politician, bureaucrat and the industrialist as also in all walks of life. According to Plato, until and unless the rulers or the person who wield power do not have the power and spirit of philosophy and political wisdom, the country will perish.

In today's information age, television, print and electronic media are vying to win over human minds with information overload. The same principle is also used by the perpetrators of terror to indoctrinate vulnerable young minds. The ability to think critically and handle the plethora of information that the human mind is tasked with is a necessity of the society in these modern times. Philosophy as mandatory part of the educational curriculum is the way ahead. Not only to prevent suicide terrorism, but also to improve the value system which is vital to the healthy development of society.

Philosophy Curriculum in Schools and the United Nations

The importance of philosophy to the work of UNESCO is evident, since philosophical analysis and reflection are undeniably linked to the establishment and maintenance of peace, the core mission of the organization. The organization's constitution provides that peace must be founded "upon the intellectual and moral solidarity of mankind". By developing the intellectual tools to analyze and understand key concepts such as justice, dignity and freedom, by building capacities for independent thought and judgment, by enhancing the critical skills to understand and question the world and its challenges, and by fostering reflection on values and principles, philosophy is a "school of freedom" (UNESCO, 2005).

UN has also laid down the vision of philosophy in education as follows. The teaching of philosophy contributes to the development of free citizens. It encourages one to judge for one, to confront all sorts of arguments, to respect what others have to say, and to submit only to the authority of reason. This in other words is a practical training in basic rights, building the capacity for individuals to have a genuine freedom of thought, freedom from dogmas and unquestioned wisdom. It also fosters the ability of human beings to make judgments concerning his/her situation. This is inevitably linked to the possibility of evaluation, critique and choice for action or non action. (UNESCO, 2004)

The UN approach to philosophy is on a broad level to achieve many of the goals laid down. Suicide terrorism has got many facets. In most cases suicide terrorists are the expendable foot soldiers. They are a means to an end in the changing cycle of violent political struggles or class struggles or may even include clash of civilizations. For that suicide terrorist, the motivation and the goals are individualistic.

The aim of introducing philosophy in school curriculum is to protect many volunteer walk in suicide terrorists from manipulative forces. The aim of this book is to sensitize the reader to this important aspect of education which can pay rich dividends to the society.

KEY WORDS AND DEFINITIONS

Key words:

Moral Ignorance, Blameless Ignorance, Culpability, Recklessness, Akrasia, Clear-eyed Akrasia and Parity thesis.

Key Definitions

Moral Ignorance: The view that one can fail to know what one ought to do in some particular case; one fail to know a general moral rule. One can fail to know that people have certain rights, or that one has certain duties. One can fail to know a certain act would be cruel or abusive and so on (Rosen, 2003, p.64).

Epistemic Obligation: The view that standing obligations to inform ourselves about matters relevant to the moral permissibility of our conduct: to look around, to reflect, to seek advice and so on i.e. moral obligations governing the epistemic aspects of deliberation (Rosen, 2003, p.63).

Akrasia: Acting against one's own better judgment.

Clear-eyed Akrasia: Acting against one's own considered judgment about what there is most reason for him to do.

REFERENCES

Bakken, N.W. (2007) The Anatomy of Suicide Terrorism: A Durkheimian Analysis. University of Delaware: International Foundation for Protection Officers.

Bird, S. (2008) 'Kafeel Ahmed, Glasgow attack terrorist who burnt to death'. *The Sunday Times.* 16 December.

Bone, J. and Hussain, Z. (2008) 'Al-Qaeda Woman 'Aafia Siddiqui' in court on attempted murder charge'. *The Sunday Times.* 6 August.

Borowitz, A. (2005) Terrorism as self-glorification: The Herostratos syndrome. Kent: Kent St. University Press.

Cam, P. (2010) 'Philosophy for a Thinking Curriculum' [online] Newton: The Philosophy in Schools Association of New South Wales.

Davidson, D. (1969) 'How is Weakness of the Will Possible?' In Davidson, D., *Essays on Actions and Events* (1980). Oxford: Oxford University Press. pp.21-42.

Executive Board of UNESCO (2005). Intersectoral Strategy on Philosophy. Adopted by the 171ˢᵗ session (Document 171EX12)

Fitzpatrick, W.J. (2008) 'Moral Responsibility and Normative Ignorance'. *Ethics.* 118: 589-613.

Guerrero, A.A. (2007) 'Don't Know, Don't Kill: Moral Ignorance, Culpability, and Caution'. *Philosophical studies* [online] **136**, 59-97. Available from: http: //philosophy.fas.nyu.edu/docs/IO/1326/DKDK. pdf. [Accessed on 14ᵗʰ August 2009]

Gunaratna, R. 'The LTTE and suicide terrorism'. *Frontline Magazine.* 05 February 2008 [online] **17** (3). Available from: http://www. hinduonnet.com/fline/fl1703/1730/17031060.htm. [Accessed on 26ᵗʰ July 2009].

Rosen, G. (2004) 'Skepticism about Moral Responsibility'. *Philosophical Perpectives*. **18**, 295-313.

Rosen, G. (2003) 'Culpability and Ignorance'. *Proceedings of the Aristotelian Society*. **103**, 61-84.

Smith, H. (1983) 'Culpable Ignorance'. *The Philosophical Review*. **92**, 543-571.

UNESCO (2004) Section of Philosophy and Human Sciences UNESCO Strategy on Philosophy DRAFT November / December.

Williams, B.G. (2007) *The Taliban Fedayeen: The World's Worst Suicide Bombers?* The Jamestown Foundation [online] **14**(5),p.2.

Zimmerman, M.J. (1997) 'Moral responsibility and ignorance'. *Ethics*. **107** (3), 410-426.

BIBLIOGRAPHY

Atwan, A.B. (2006) Secret History of Al Qaeda. California: University of California Press.

Dr. Sharma, Ramnath. (2005) History of western Philosophy. Meerut: India Kedarnath Ramnath.

Goldman, A.I. (2006) Stimulating Minds. New York: Oxford University Press.

Herbert Bix (2000) Hirohito and the Making of Modern Japan, HarperCollins; 1ˢᵗ Edition (August 22, 2000).

Lal B.K. (2005) Contemporary Indian Philosophy, Delhi: Motilal Banarasi Dass Printers

Lapierre, D. and Collins, L. (2007) Freedom at Midnight. Mumbai: Vikas Publishing House Pvt. Ltd.

Mcdermott, T. (2005) Perfect soldiers: The 9/11 Hijackers; who they were, why they did it. U.S.A: HarperCollins.

Neill, S. O. and McGrory, D. (2006) The Suicide Factory. London: Harper Collins Publishers.

Pape, R.A. (2005) Dying to win: The Strategic Logic of Suicide Terrorism. United States: Random House.

Peters, E. (1989) Inquisition. California: University of California Press.

Peterson, M., Hasker, W., Reichenbach, B., Basinger, D. (2007) *Philosophy of Religion.* 3ʳᵈ Edition. New York: Oxford University Press.

Rolland, R. (2007) The World Religion of Vivekananda Whose Time is Now. New Delhi: Vijay Goel.

Willheim, R. (1999) Emotion, Evaluation and Rationality. York University Press.

Smith, M. (1994) The Moral Problem. U.S.A.: Blackwell Publishing.

Strawson, P. (1982) Freedom and Resentment, reprinted in: Watson, G. (2007) *Free Will*. 2nd Edition. New York: Oxford University Press.

Sharma, R. (1982) Philosophy of Religion. New Delhi: Kedar Nath Ram Nath.

Sharma, C. (2003) A critical survey of Indian Philosophy. Delhi: Motilal Banarsi Dass Publishers.

Wallace, R.J. (1994) Responsibility and the Moral Sentiments. Cambridge MA: Harvard University Press.

Watson, G. (1982) Free Will. New York: Oxford University Press.

Wilber, K. (2007) The integral vision: A very short introduction to the revolutionary integral approach to life, god, the universe and everything for a thorough, accessible introduction to AQAL metatheory.

Wilson, C. (1984) A criminal history of mankind. New York: Granada Publishing Limited. P.172

ABOUT THE AUTHOR

K.C. ELDHO

K.C. Eldho, born on 30th May 1965 as a Syrian Jacobite Christian at Kangarapady near Thrikkakara, Ernakulam District is the youngest son of late K V Chakkappan a businessman and Mariamma Chakkappan a retired school teacher belonging to Kochery family. Eldho is an alumnus of Maharajas College, Ernakulam. He completed his bachelor degree in Philosophy and was the 1st rank holder in the stream. He obtained his Law degree in 1991 and Masters in Philosophy in 1993 from University of Kerala and was conferred Master of Research in Philosophy from the University of Manchester in 2009. In 2010, on a special invite, he attended the World Conference on prevention of Terrorism at the

London Olympia. Eldho is a regular columnist in various law journals. He is a litigating lawyer in the High Court of Kerala ever since 1992 and is the founding managing partner of BC 370 Law Associates, a full service law firm.

Suicide Terrorism—A Solution is his first book.

www.ingramcontent.com/pod-product-compliance
Lightning Source LLC
Chambersburg PA
CBHW050426290526
45786CB00003B/1408